INTRODUCTION TO BLOCKCHAIN TECHNOLOGY

Other publications by Van Haren Publishing

Van Haren Publishing (VHP) specializes in titles on Best Practices, methods and standards within four domains:
- IT and IT Management
- Architecture (Enterprise and IT)
- Business Management and
- Project Management

Van Haren Publishing is also publishing on behalf of leading organizations and companies: ASLBiSL Foundation, BRMI, CA, Centre Henri Tudor, Gaming Works, IACCM, IAOP, IFDC, Innovation Value Institute, IPMA-NL, ITSqc, NAF, KNVI, PMI-NL, PON, The Open Group, The SOX Institute.

Topics are (per domain):

IT and IT Management	**Enterprise Architecture**	**Project Management**
ABC of ICT	ArchiMate®	A4-Projectmanagement
ASL®	GEA®	DSDM/Atern
CATS CM®	Novius Architectuur	ICB / NCB
CMMI®	Methode	ISO 21500
COBIT®	TOGAF®	MINCE®
e-CF		M_o_R®
ISO/IEC 20000	**Business Management**	MSP®
ISO/IEC 27001/27002	*BABOK® Guide*	P3O®
ISPL	BiSL® and BiSL® Next	*PMBOK® Guide*
IT4IT®	BRMBOK™	Praxis®
IT-CMF™	BTF	PRINCE2®
IT Service CMM	EFQM	
ITIL®	eSCM	
MOF	IACCM	
MSF	ISA-95	
SABSA	ISO 9000/9001	
SAF	OPBOK	
SIAM™	SixSigma	
TRIM	SOX	
VeriSM™	SqEME®	

For the latest information on VHP publications, visit our website: www.vanharen.net.

Introduction to blockchain technology

The many faces of blockchain technology in the 21st century

Tiana Laurence

Colophon

Title:	Introduction to blockchain technology
Subtitle:	The many faces of blockchain technology in the 21st century
Author:	Tiana Laurence
Reviewers:	Atul Anand (Global MBA, SP Jain: Strategic Management, IIMC) Stefan Macica (Slovakia) Rita Pilon (EXIN) Scott Robinson (founder of Plug and Play FinTech) Mikulas Zalai (Slovakia)
Text editor:	Steve Newton
Publisher:	Van Haren Publishing, 's-Hertogenbosch, www.vanharen.net
ISBN Hard copy:	978 94 018 0499 8
ISBN eBook pdf:	978 94 018 0501 8
ISBN eBook EPUB:	978 94 018 0504 9
Edition:	First edition, first impression, October 2019
Layout and DTP:	Coco Bookmedia, Amersfoort – NL
Copyright:	© Van Haren Publishing, 2019

Nothing from this publication may be reproduced, recorded in an automated database or published on or via any medium, either electronically, mechanically, through photocopying or any other method, without prior written permission from the publisher.

This publication was produced with the utmost care and attention. Nevertheless, the text may contain errors. The publisher and the authors are not liable for any errors and/or inaccuracies in this text.

Preface

Dear reader,

You have heard buzz words like "bitcoin", "blockchain", and "cryptocurrency". They are everywhere. Companies and governments have started to use blockchain technology in earnest and will increasingly do so for the foreseeable future. It is time to take an in-depth look at blockchain technology, and how you can take advantage of its potential.

This book is perfect for you if you are looking to expand your knowledge of blockchain technology but are not a programmer. It is about software but not written for technical experts. It assumes that you have little to no knowledge of the subject and will explain topics as simply as possible, while not obscuring details that may affect you. The book will give you insight into the critical differences in blockchain software and will provide you with a basic understanding of how and why they work.

After reading this volume, you will be able to speak with confidence on the topic, know key differences in technology, and why they are relevant to you, your company, and your industry. You will also have critical insight into blockchain software's inherent limitations and shortcomings.

The popularization of blockchain has shrouded the sector into the realm of alchemy. Attaching the words "tokenization" and "blockchain" have spontaneously transformed the mundane into the magical. This book will demystify the topic and cut through the hype. You will understand the changes that are happening and uncover any pretense.

In this book, each chapter ends with review questions to help you better understand the core of the chapter.

I hope you will enjoy this book.

Kind regards,

Tiana Laurence

VI

Contents

1	**Introduction to Blockchain Technology**	**1**
	1.1 Key blockchain concepts	1
	What is a blockchain?	2
	What are nodes?	4
	What is cryptocurrency?	9
	What are tokens?	10
	What does distributed mean?	11
	1.2 Summary	14
	1.3 Test your knowledge	14
2	**Key parts of blockchain technology**	**17**
	2.1 Cryptography	17
	Machines that encrypted data in the past	17
	Modern encryption	18
	Private and public keys	18
	2.2 What is a hash?	19
	From blocks to hashes	20
	2.3 Ledgers	21
	Transactions and trade	21
	2.4 The public witness	22
	Computers that witness	23
	2.5 Summary	27
	2.6 Test your knowledge	28
3	**The structure of the network: consensus algorithm**	**31**
	3.1 Proof of Work	31
	3.2 Proof of Stake (PoS)	33
	3.3 Delegated Proof of Stake	34
	3.4 Proof of Authority	35
	3.5 Proof of Elapsed Time	36
	3.6 Proof of Capacity and Proof of Space	37
	3.7 Proof of Burn	38
	3.8 Hyperledger Fabric	39
	3.9 Summary	40
	3.10 Test your knowledge	41
4	**Key blockchain networks and technologies**	**45**
	4.1 The history of blockchain networks	46
	4.2 Top challenges for blockchain networks	47
	4.3 A deeper dive into Bitcoin	48
	The top challenges that face Bitcoin's global adoption	49
	Major Bitcoin contributors	50

	4.4	Hyperledger	51
	4.5	EOS's delegated Proof of Stake	53
	4.6	Ripple	55
	4.7	Unearthing Ethereum	59
	4.8	The Waves platform – a Russian blockchain	62
	4.9	Summary	64
	4.10	Test your knowledge	65

5 Second generation applications of Blockchain technology — 69

	5.1	Smart contracts	69
		Smart contracts: origins and how they function	70
		Creating and deploying smart contracts	71
	5.2	Tokens	72
		Token standards	73
		Second generation tokens	74
	5.3	Decentralized applications	74
		How are DApps constructed?	75
	5.4	Decentralized Autonomous Organizations (DAOs)	76
		How DAOs work	78
		Key takeaways about DAOs	78
		Legality of DAOs	79
	5.5	Summary	79
	5.6	Test your knowledge	79

6 Expanding applications of blockchain — 83

	6.1	Decentralized identity	83
		Online identity - the honey pot	83
		Self-sovereign identity	84
		What is identity?	85
		History of identity documentation	86
		Challenges of identity	87
	6.2	Blockchain protected identity	88
		Blockstack	89
		Microsoft	89
		IBM's Trusted Identity	89
		Civic	90
	6.3	Blockchain and IoT	90
		Toyota	91
		IBM	92
	6.4	Artificial Intelligence and blockchain	92
		The history of Artificial Intelligence	93
		Companies building blockchain technology for AI	93
		SingularityNET	94
		Enigma	94
		Matrix AI network	94

6.5	Decentralized marketplaces and exchanges	94
	Challenges of decentralized marketplaces	96
	Lack of legal framework	96
	Emerging developments	96
	Loss of customer touch	97
	Popular decentralized marketplaces and exchanges	97
	OpenBazaar	97
	ModulTrade	97
	FundRequest	97
6.6	Summary	98
6.7	Test your knowledge	98

7 Blockchain and the world economy — 101

7.1	Supply chain industry	101
	Supply chain of the past	102
	Supply chain of the future	102
	Supply chain using blockchain technology	103
7.2	Cross-border money transfer	105
	A little history in cross-border money transfer	105
	Innovation in cross-border payment	106
	Cross-border payment of the future	106
	Top three challenges in cross-border money transfer	107
7.3	Financial change agents	108
	The Ripple protocol	108
	The R3 consortium	109
	COTI	109
	Everex	109
	SendFriend	110
7.4	Summary	110
7.5	Test your knowledge	110

8 New frontiers in blockchain and business — 113

8.1	Digital fiat currency	113
	History of digital fiat currency	114
	Top challenges in the digital fiat currency industry	115
	Long-term effects to physical tenders	115
8.2	Disrupters in banking and currency	115
	eCurrency	116
	Blockstream - Liquid	116
	Ripio	116
	Woorton	116
	BABB	117

	8.3	Blockchain and insurance	117
		History of insurance	118
		Insurance of the present	118
		Insurance of the future	118
		Top challenges in the insurance industry	118
		Blockchain startup companies in the insurance industry	119
		Black	119
		BlockRe	119
		B3i	120
		ChainThat	120
	8.4	Intellectual property rights and providence	120
		History of intellectual property rights	121
		Intellectual property at present	121
		Intellectual property of the future	122
		Top challenges in the intellectual property rights industry	122
		Digital reproduction	122
		Coverage expansion of rights	122
		Digital IP of the future	122
		IPwe	123
		LOCI	123
		Vaultitude	124
	8.5	Summary	124
	8.6	Test your knowledge	125

9 Blockchain and people — 129

	9.1	Lean governments	129
	9.2	Estonia's e-Residency	130
	9.3	Better authentication and notarization in China	131
	9.4	The trust layer for the internet	131
	9.5	Spam-free email	131
	9.6	Blockchain oracles for IoT	132
	9.7	IP and trusted authorship	133
	9.8	Intellectual property rights	133
	9.9	Government	135
		Smart cities of China - Hangzhou	135
		U.S. Department of Homeland Security	135
		Singapore's Smart Nation project	136
		Singapore satellite cities in India	136
		China's Whole Country strategy	137
	9.10	Financial capitals of the world	137
		London	138
		Exciting projects across the UK	138

9.11	Dubai's 2020 goal	138
9.12	BitLicense of New York City	139
9.13	Malta, the blockchain island of the EU	140
9.14	German blockchain	140
9.15	French blockchain efforts	141
9.16	Summary	141
9.17	Test your knowledge	142

10 Blockchain and the inhibitors — 143

10.1	Blockchain vulnerabilities	143
	Smart contract vulnerabilities	143
	Centralized public networks	144
	Centralized private networks	145
10.2	Community fractures and feuds	145
10.3	Fraud and scams	146
	Advanced fee schemes	147
	Identity theft and credit card fraud	147
	Internet and device hacking	147
	Market manipulation	148
	Pyramid and Ponzi schemes	149
10.4	Summary	150
10.5	Test your knowledge	150

Appendix A: Answer Keys — 153

Index — 155

1 Introduction to Blockchain Technology

Blockchain has become an omnipresent term that encompasses a social promise and a new technology. Originally proposed as a solution for Bitcoin's cryptocurrency record keeping system, blockchains are now used to store the records of all types of applications.

Blockchain means something more in many people's minds. The promise many associate with blockchain applications is that they will collapse all centralized systems. Centralized systems are everywhere people need to trust a counterparty and don't have the resources themselves to do so independently.

An easy way to identify a place where blockchain technology may be applied is to look for areas where a middleman is needed to facilitate trust. Trust is essential for things such as the transfer of money, voting, land records, IP rights, and identity. Blockchain software can be programmed to take the place of the middleman by becoming the trusted record keeping system.

In this chapter, you will learn the basics of blockchain software. This includes the vital concepts that govern most blockchains, economic models, and network structures. It will help you lay a strong foundation for understanding how the technology works and what it is capable of doing.

1.1 Key blockchain concepts

Blockchain technology has come a long way since the initial vision published by Satoshi Nakamoto in the Bitcoin white paper in 2008. Buzz words like "bitcoin", "blockchain", and "cryptocurrency" are everywhere. Companies and governments have started to use blockchain technology in earnest and will increasingly do so for the foreseeable future.

Since its initial conception, blockchain has encompassed both a social promise and new technology. Originally proposed as a solution for Bitcoin's cryptocurrency record-keeping system, blockchains are now used to store the records of all types of applications.

Core services you may depend on every day such as the transfer of money, payments, voting, land records, IP rights, and identity all rely on intermediaries. Blockchain software has begun taking the place of these antiquated systems. The software becomes the trusted record-keeping systems, and the rules programed into the software become the intermediaries.

It is important to note that blockchains can be used for more than just recording the transfer of value between two parties. The primary benefits of cryptographic identity, historical and chronological provenance, and the transparency of the networks complete history work exceptionally well for many industries that require two parties to trust each other.

Pigeonholing blockchain technology solely for financial transactions is a very limited perspective. Before you can fully grasp the potential applications of blockchains as part of a technology stack, it's important to understand how the technology works. In the following section you will learn about the key concepts that make blockchain technology revolutionary.

What is a blockchain?

Blockchain technology structure was first described in the Bitcoin white paper as a peer-to-peer distributed time-stamp server. The author, Satoshi Nakamoto (possibly a fictitious name), wanted to create a peer-to-peer electronic cash system that did not need a network of banks to operate. Satoshi described "blocks" and "chains" as a way of organizing and securing records, such that once entries had been made into a shared database, they could be proved mathematically correct and to have remained unchanged.

Satoshi's description of blocks are groups of transactions that have occurred over a period of time. A transaction, in the case of Bitcoin, represents the transfer of some cryptocurrency, known as bitcoin, from one user to another.

For example, Sally sends you a bitcoin, you receive it, and the transfer of the bitcoin between the two of you is recorded as a "transaction". Bob, Joe, Mark, and Tammy send each other bitcoins at the same time. All of these transactions are bundled into a block and are recorded in the Bitcoin blockchain.

Blockchains have a special way of recording the transfer of bitcoins from one party to another. The transactions are time-stamped and signed by the sender of the bitcoin. So, in the example above, Sally signs the transfer of bitcoin to you. Sally's signature for the transfer of bitcoin is not an ink and paper kind. Sally signs electronically or rather cryptographically, with what is called a private key. What this means is that the blockchain software can tell she and no one else has the authority to transfer that bitcoin.

Once Sally's transaction with you has been recorded in the block with all the other bitcoin transfers, the block is sealed and linked to the other blocks of transactions. Blocks are sealed and linked by hashes. Hashes are created through a cryptographic hash function.

How hash functions are used in blockchains is very clever but simple. All the data that make up a block of transactions are processed. The output of this mathematical process is a string of numbers and letters of a fixed-size, for Bitcoin it is 32 bytes. If the input does not change, the hash function will always result in the same output string. Hash functions are a covenant way in computer science to prove data has not changed.

Once a hash has been generated from a block, the fixed string of numbers and letters is recorded in the next new block of transactions. Recording the hash of the previous block of transactions links one block to another chronologically. Removing a block, or even a single

Introduction to Blockchain Technology

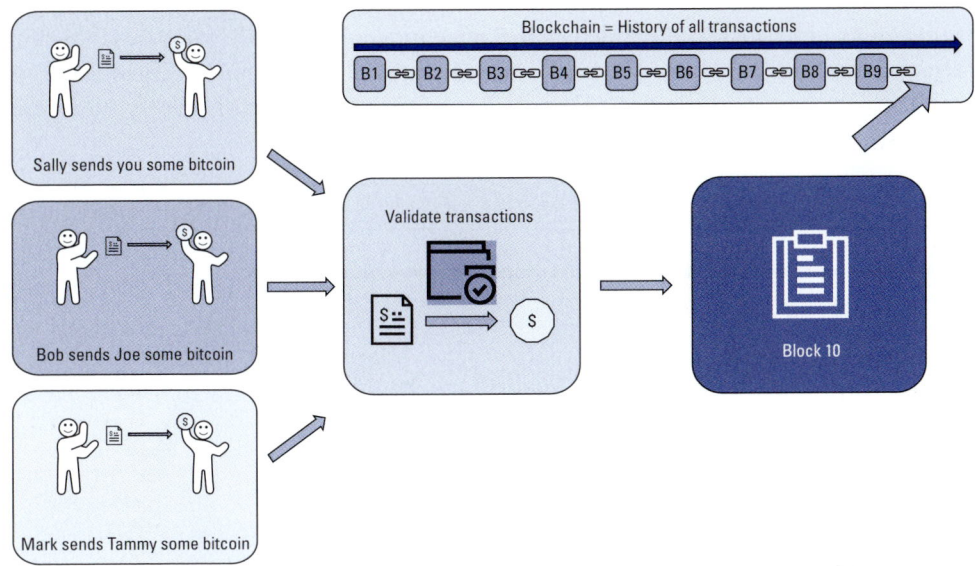

Figure 1   What is a blockchain?

transaction, from within a block would break the record and would instantly be noticeable to everyone, as your fixed string of 32 characters would not match their fixed string. See figure 2.

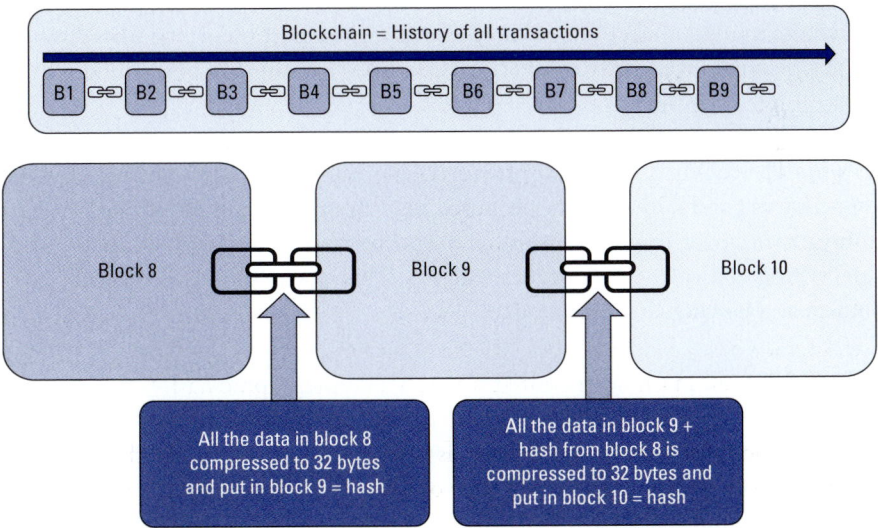

Figure 2   Hash function in blocks of transactions.

Satoshi's goal was to prevent Sally from sending the same bitcoin to you and someone else and thus defrauding the network. The "block" and "chain" of blockchain technology is a clever way of structuring and recording transaction data chronologically. It keeps track of "who" owns "what" and "when".

The Bitcoin white paper incorporated an incentive program for participants to process new transactions and to keep an unaltered record of every past transaction. In Bitcoin, this incentive system is called mining, and the incentive given to the miners is the cryptocurrency bitcoin, see figure 3.

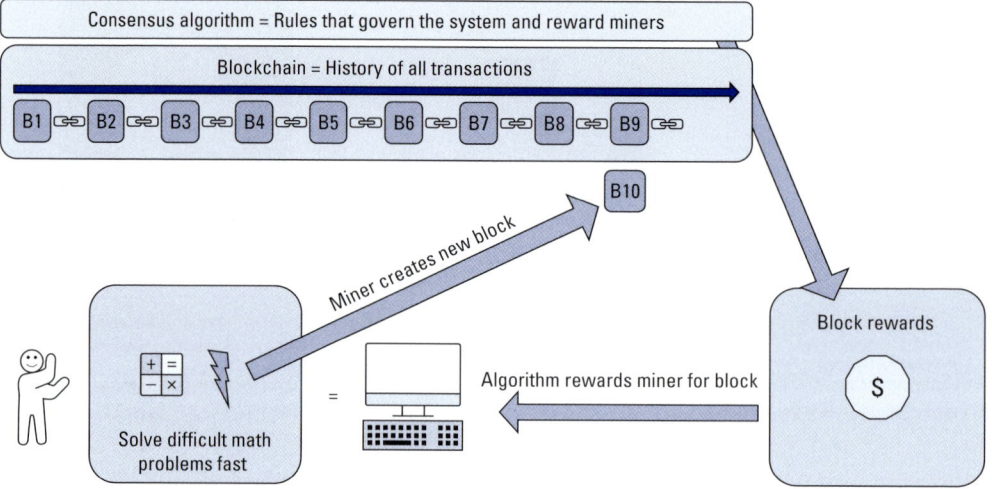

Figure 3   The concept of mining.

Satoshi understood that if a single person or entity had master editing power over the records, then the transaction could be altered, defeating the purpose. If the record was broken, then it may be possible for Sally to send you and Bob the same bitcoin.

Satoshi, possibly inspired by the financial crisis of 2008, wanted to stop fraudulent transactions without needing a third party to aggregate records and provide trust that everyone would operate in good faith. Satoshi proposed that the aggregation of records could be done with software via a peer-to-peer distributed time-stamp server and trust could be established through cryptographically-provable mathematics. This system of record keeping is what you now known as a blockchain.

What are nodes?
When a computer connects to a blockchain network, the computer becomes a *node*. A node runs the blockchain software for the network and keeps the network healthy by engaging in the transfer of information. Anyone can run a node on a public network like Bitcoin. Nodes broadcast bitcoin transactions to other nodes throughout the network. However, not all nodes are the same.

There are several classifications of nodes depending on the level of participation and the type of blockchain network. Every network has different roles available. For example, when you run a node that has a complete history of the network's transactions and verifies all of the rules of the system, it is called a *full node*. Full nodes download every block, and then they check each transaction and block to make sure they are compliant with the rules of the network. The network's rules are called its *consensus system*. See figure 4.

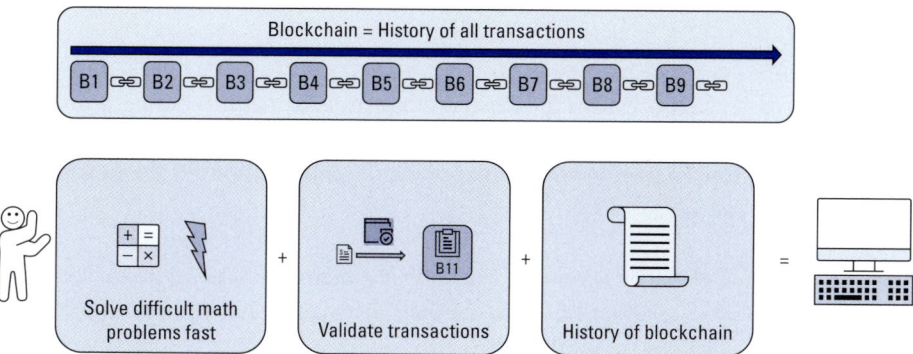

Figure 4   What is a node?

Every blockchain has unique consensus rules. These rules cover things like the number of cryptocurrency units rewarded to miners and how transactions and blocks are formatted. When a full node finds a transaction or block that breaks the consensus rules, the node rejects the transaction or the block. Each full node works independently.

Operating a full node can be resource-intensive. It requires downloading every transaction for the full history of that blockchain. Full nodes need all new transaction records. They keep all *block headers*. Block headers identify a unique block and contain a hash of the previous block. All of this data adds up and takes up a lot of room. The Bitcoin blockchain is hundreds of gigabytes in size and growing every day.

However, there is a way to connect to a blockchain, without committing as many resources to the network. This is called a *lightweight node* or *client*. Lightweight nodes verify transactions by piggybacking on the work of full nodes. They only download the headers of all blocks and then check transactions utilizing a system called Simplified Payment Verification (SPV). As you may remember, the block headers contain hashes that prove that each block is in order and has all its transactions.

Operating a lightweight node may seem appealing. However, they are vulnerable to being tricked by bad actors. Because the SVP method is only checking the blockchain header, the lightweight node may accept transactions or blocks that are not valid. If you think you have received some bitcoin for example, but in reality you have not, this could cause financial issues. Full nodes provide the highest protection from fraud related to the transfer of cryptocurrency.

Another common way to connect to a blockchain network is to mine. A *miner* is a type of node that is adding transactions to new blocks. Miners compete to win the right to create a new complete block by solving a complex mathematical problem. Each miner will write their answer in the block header and if they are correct, they are then rewarded with cryptocurrency. The problem that miners are trying to solve is to guess a number that, when combined with the hashed transaction data from the block, returns an answer that is within a specific range called a "nonce". For Bitcoin, a nonce is a number between 0 and 4,294,967,296.

The first miner to get a hash within the desired range broadcasts the winning number to the rest of the network. All the other miners promptly stop their work on that block and start guessing the nonce for the next block. At that point the competition for the next new block begins.

Miners opt into the ruleset by accepting the software upgrades. The network has available upgrades that users elect to adopt by updating their software. You can think of the upgrades as software patches. The upgrades are only as good as the acceptance and use by the miners. There are three critical distinctions in blockchain nodes that are worth understanding as these affect the assumptions that are made around fairness, censorship, and permanence of data.

Public blockchain nodes

Public blockchains are open to anyone in the world to participate in the functions of the network, only limited by their access to the internet, hardware, and electricity. This means that you can be a miner earning cryptocurrency as your secure blocks, a full node checking transactions, or a lightweight node sending and receiving messages on the network. There are no gating mechanisms, no one to ask permission and no licensing fee. The software is held in an open license such as the Apache or MIT license. Prominent examples of this type of network include Bitcoin and Ethereum.

Permissioned blockchain nodes

Permissioned blockchains are private networks that utilize some blockchain technology but not all. Most don't incorporate any kind of mining and so do not have a native cryptocurrency. This means that there are no disinterested third parties securing blocks, the blocks and transactions are all processed by known participants. The participants all have a vested interest in the integrity of the records. Often these networks are built by for-profit companies and are operated by consortiums such as R3.

Nodes on a Corda network

R3 (www.r3cev.com) built a consortium with more than 100 of the world's leading banks and insurance companies. They work to streamline redundant business processes by integrating blockchain technology.

Corda is the blockchain protocol behind R3. It is a distributed ledger platform, often referred to as "DLT" (distributed ledger technology). Breaking down the jargon, a "ledger" is a general term for describing records used to account for something and "distributed" means that the record is kept in more than one location. It is designed specifically to manage and synchronize financial agreements between regulated financial institutions.

The R3 platform works very differently from public blockchains. There is no mining, and the transmission of data is not public in the same sense as it is on platforms such as Ethereum or Bitcoin. Unlike public blockchains that broadcast their transactions to the whole network, transactions execute in parallel on different nodes. Each node is unaware of the other's transactions. The history of each network is on a need-to-know basis and cannot be viewed by the public.

Key features of Corda include the following:
- Controlled access to the network;
- Observer node for regulators;
- Transactions are validated only by the parties involved;
- Compatible with multiple consensus mechanisms;
- No mining and no cryptocurrency.

Nodes on a Hyperledger Fabric network
Nodes on Hyperledger Fabric (see also: https://www.hyperledger.org/projects/fabric) are called Peers and Orderers. Unlike public blockchains that have nodes validating transactions or mining, the nodes on Fabric host the ledger's data and make sure it's in order. The data they host may include smart contracts, orderers, policies, channels, applications, organizations, identities, and membership. Another important distinction is that a Fabric peer can host more than one blockchain ledger. This feature allows for flexible architecture in the design of your private blockchain system.

Blockchain applications connect with peers on Fabric through APIs, application programming interfaces. The APIs allow you to invoke Fabric smart contracts in order to create transactions. Once you have submitted your transaction, they will be ordered and committed to Fabric. This does not just happen right away. The transaction must get approval from enough peers before the ledger is changed. It is possible to have two or more peers agree to cooperate privately. In Fabric this is called a *channel*. In the channel, the peers agree to collaborate to share and manage identical copies of the ledger associated with their channel.

Otherwise, when you submit a transaction, there is a three-phase process. This process ensures all peers keep their ledgers consistent with each other, see figure 5. This is where orderer peers are important. Their job is to ensure that every peer's ledger is kept consistent. Single peers cannot update the ledger by themselves.

- Phase 1: an update to the ledger is requested by a blockchain application. Peers will endorse the transaction. Once a transaction has gained enough endorsements, the transaction will move to phase 2.

- Phase 2: the endorsed transactions are collected together and packaged into blocks. The orderer is crucial to this process. Peer audit by an orderer ensures this is done correctly.

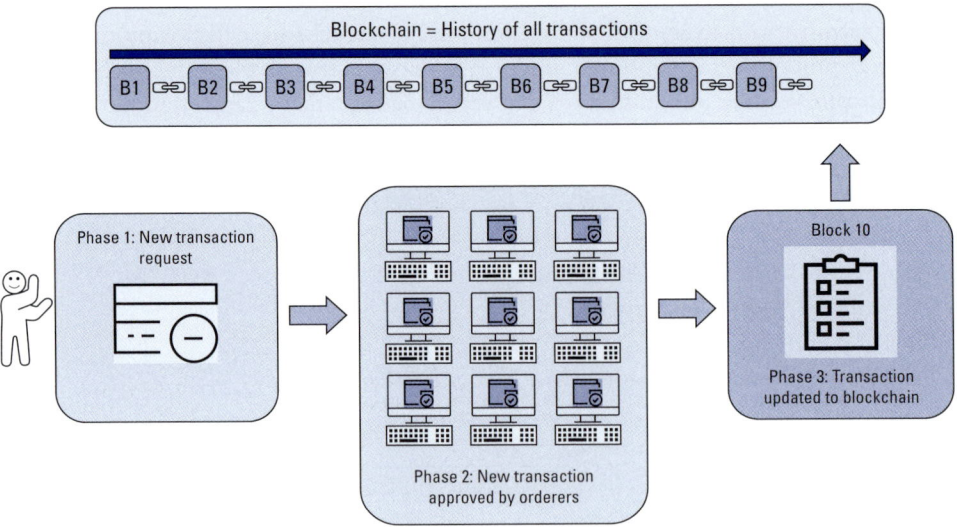

Figure 5   The Fabric three-phase process.

- Phase 3: the new block that was created is broadcast back to every peer so that they can update their blockchain record. Each transaction in the new block is then validated by the peer before being applied to its copy of the ledger.

Federated blockchain nodes

Federated blockchain nodes can exist in both public blockchains and private blockchains. Federation is when the system, or rather the user of a system, elect nodes to process transactions. Designating a few nodes to do most of the work of maintaining the blockchain records has its advantages and disadvantages.

One of the main reasons why systems choose this type of architecture is because it can reduce the raw cost of processing transactions and it can increase the speed at which the blockchain is updated and transactions are cleared.

However, there are some very good reasons to not have federated nodes. Blockchains are often judged to be less resilient to corruption when they have fewer nodes operating and securing the network. It is more feasible to take over a handful of computers and their operators then it is the ten thousand or more nodes that operate at any given time on the Bitcoin network.

Here are a few examples of blockchain networks that operate with some form of federation or designated nodes.

Factom is a public blockchain that has two classes of federated nodes, see figure 6. Half of these are processing transactions whilst the other half watch to make sure that the nodes processing the transactions are accurate and not censoring transactions. Users of the system elect nodes to be Federated Factom nodes. Factom does not use mining but does have a native cryptocurrency. The Federated nodes are rewarded with "Factoids" the Factom cryptocurrency for processing transactions. The nodes can then sell Factoids back into the market to those who wish to utilize the Factom blockchain.

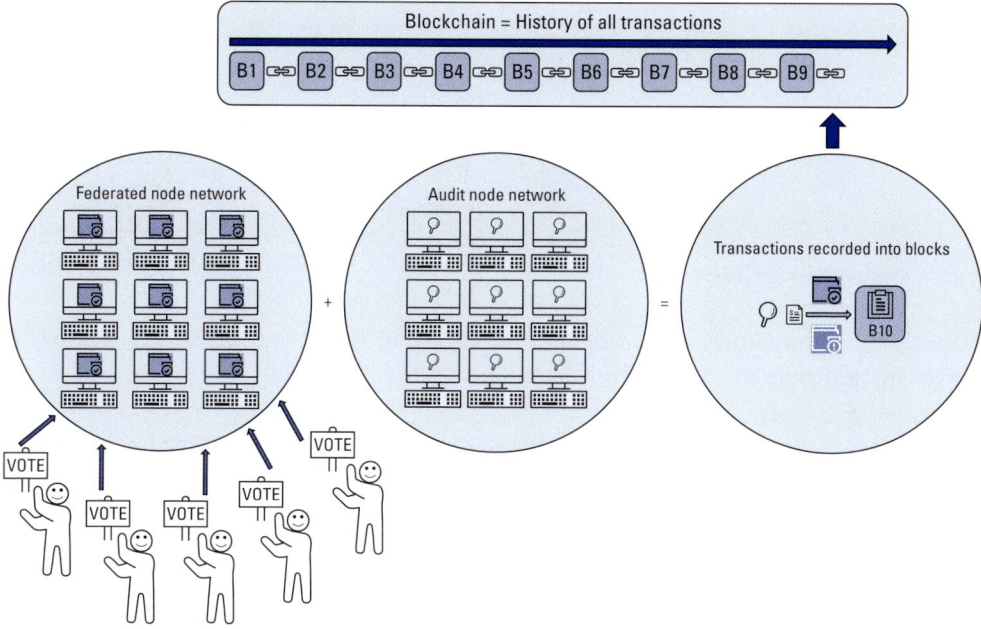

Figure 6   The Factom federated network.

Waves is a public blockchain that limits participation in the network to nodes that hold sufficient "waves" of cryptocurrency. Currently, the limit is set to approximately 1,000 waves. The Waves blockchain is a peer-to-peer network, and any computer running the Waves software is considered a node and can propose new transactions. But only full nodes are allowed administrative duties. They relay blocks and transactions to miners and answer queries for end users about the state of the blockchain. Full nodes ensure that new blocks are valid. They check the format of the block in order to validate that all hashes in the new block are correct, that there is a hash of the previous block, and each transaction was signed by the right parties. Full nodes can mine new blocks. Mining on Waves consists only of generating new blocks, it does not require solving difficult math problems like Bitcoin. See figure 7.

What is cryptocurrency?
Cryptocurrency is a type of digital cash and is a bearer instrument. An old type of bearer instrument was a document that entitled the holder to the rights of ownership, such as shares, bonds, and cash money (coins and notes). Many bearer instruments are banned because of their potential for abuse, for example through tax evasion and money laundering.

The idea of digital cash has been around since the '90s, such as Digicash. But it never took off because all the systems relied on a trusted third party to facilitate the record of ownership

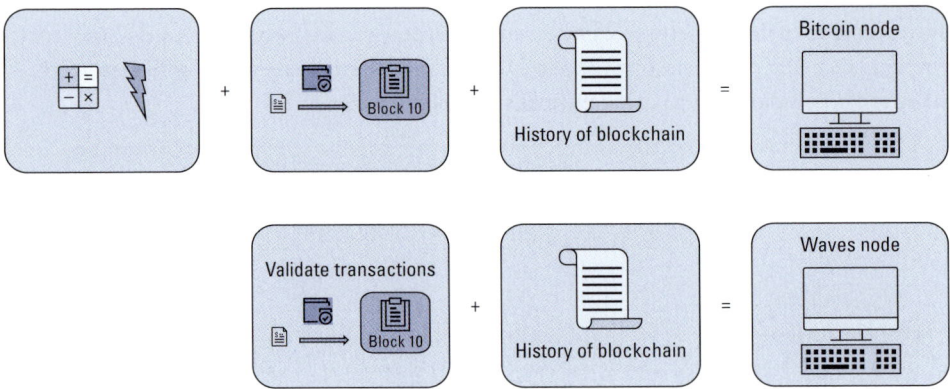

Figure 7 Bitcoin node vs. Waves node.

and transfer. A third party that facilitates the record of digital cash makes it a non-bearer instrument and gives the third party a lot of power.

Cryptocurrency was developed by Satoshi Nakamoto as a way to prevent the holder of digital currency from sending it to more than one party. This is often referred to as "preventing double-spending". In a centralized system, preventing double-spending is easy: the third party, for instance a bank, checks their record of ownership and disregards any fraudulent transfers.

The revolution that Satoshi began with Bitcoin in 2008 is a system that allowed the electronic transfer of digital cash without a central party checking its record of ownership. Satoshi developed a peer-to-peer electronic cash system.

The network collaboratively works to prevent double-spending and operates in much the same way as a network for file sharing. Every peer in the network has a list with all the network's transactions. The peers check all new transactions to make sure they are valid and that there are no attempts to double spend the cryptocurrency.

A cryptocurrency is only a valid entry in a database. Cryptography is used to ensure a request to update the database is correct. There is a distributed network that enforces the rules around updating entries. Some blockchain networks have scarcity mechanisms such as mining that drive the perceived value of an entry. But the root of any cryptocurrency is to have only a valid entry in a database. Cryptocurrencies now have real-world value and can be traded for traditional currencies or directly for goods and services.

What are tokens?

Not all blockchain networks have cryptocurrency, but all networks allow for the issuance of some kind of token. A token - much like cryptocurrency - can act as a bearer instrument and be used to transfer value between two parties over a blockchain network. It's important to note that tokens are very flexible and may not be bearer instruments.

A significant difference between a cryptocurrency and a token is who actually creates them, see figure 8. A token is created by a single party that would like to account for something of value. In contrast, a blockchain network generates a cryptocurrency as a reward mechanism for nodes that facilitate the upkeep of the shared database.

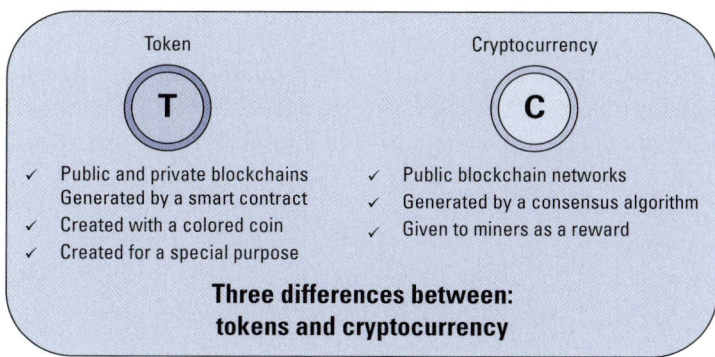

Figure 8   Differences between tokens and cryptocurrency.

The Ethereum foundation pioneered and greatly improved token technology. The Ethereum blockchain was designed to host smart contracts, and these are well suited for creating tokens. A smart contract is code that executes within a blockchain. The smart contract code is a series of instructions that dictate how that token works.

There are many types of tokens, and the Ethereum network has many standards based around how these tokens work. The shared standards allow any tokens on Ethereum to be utilized by other applications. Here are two popular token standards:

ERC-20
The ERC-20 token standard is the most popular token on the Ethereum network, and other blockchains have adopted the same rule set for their tokens. One of the driving factors for its popularity was that the ERC-20 tokens were used for crowdfunding. These funding events were called initial coin offering (ICO).

ERC-721
The ERC-721 is another popular token standard. It differs from the ERC-20 in that each token is unique. A common use for the ERC-721 is digital collectibles. It allows an issuer to prove uniqueness and transferability of a digital asset while allowing each asset to be unique. Cryptokitties (https://www.cryptokitties.co) was the first ERC-721 implementation.

What does distributed mean?
There are three main types of blockchains, as shown in figure 9:
- public blockchains,
- private blockchains, and
- hybrids.

Public blockchains allow anyone to participate in the network as long as they have access to the internet, hardware and electricity. Private blockchains only allow trusted parties to operate their blockchain. Hybrid blockchains control who can participate and at what level of participation each node is allowed to operate. These key differences are important to understand as they affect how distributed a blockchain network can become.

Distribution is characterized by how many independent nodes are operating on a network and keeping a full history of their respective blockchain. For public blockchain this would include all nodes that are mining new blocks and all nodes that are validating transactions.

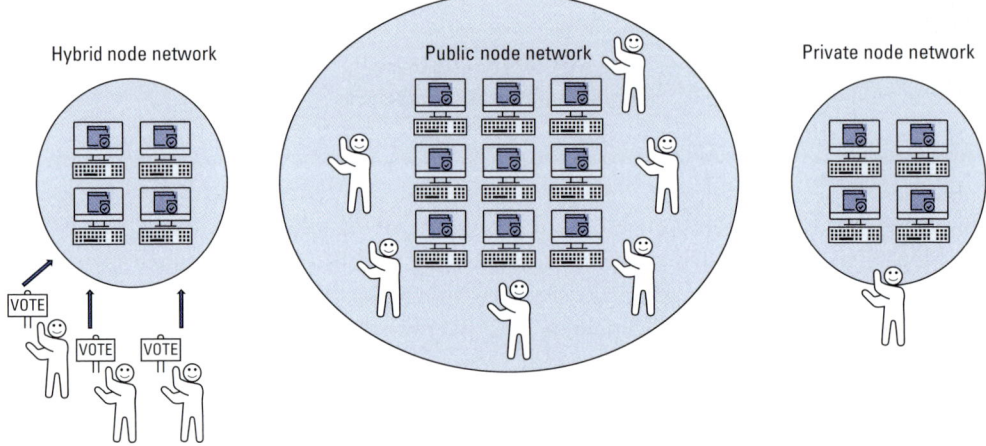

Figure 9   Hybrid, public and private networks.

A key driver in the distribution of full nodes is economic incentivization. Those blockchains where an individual makes a profit from operating as a miner or processing transactions have more full nodes. Public blockchains offer up their native cryptocurrency as a reward to those who are maintaining the network.

The fair market value of a cryptocurrency will determine how many individuals will compete to maintain the network. The market value is driven by speculation, scarcity and utility. Bitcoin, for example, has fluctuated in price wildly (see figure 10) and so has the number of independent full nodes.

Distribution is a very important consideration when picking a network to work with. The greater the number of full independent nodes, the harder it is to compromise the data that has been written into that blockchain. The greater the number of full nodes, the more difficult it is to censor data from being written into a blockchain.

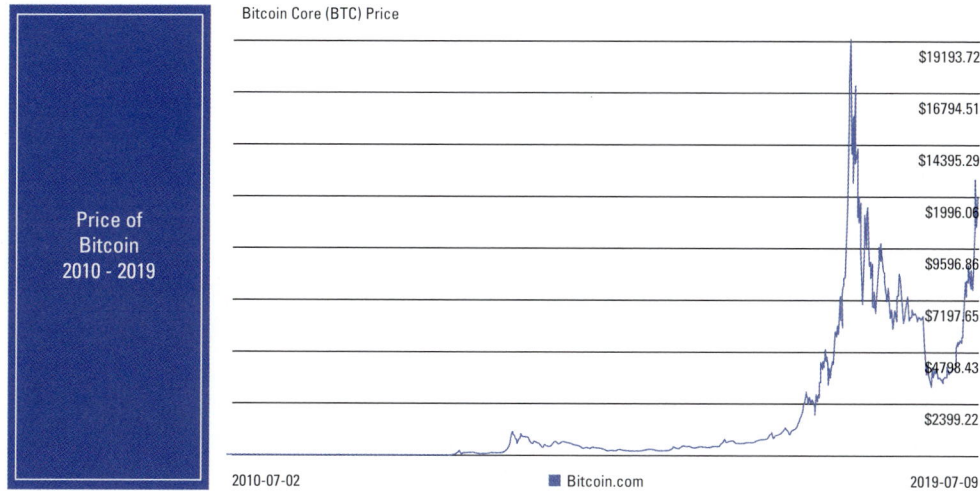

Figure 10   Price volatility of cryptocurrency.

Public blockchains that do not attract enough nodes are vulnerable to attack. Primarily, the attacker is looking to corrupt the transaction history so that they can spend a token or cryptocurrency twice. This is called a "51% attack", see figure 11. Given that blockchains have one job, making permanent data, 51% attacks create an existential threat.

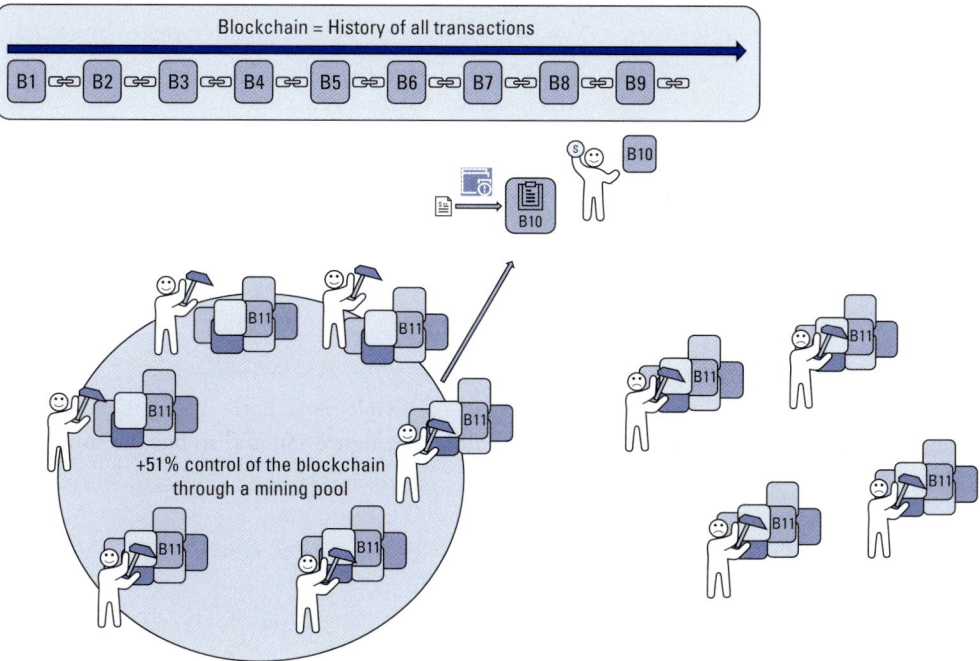

Figure 11   51% attack.

Private and hybrid blockchains combat 51% attacks by gating full node access to only known parties. However, they are exposed to just the same problem from within. A few hybrid blockchains have created workarounds where they publish a hash of their network every so often into a highly distributed public blockchain. This hash is called a Merkle tree root and allows a hybrid blockchain to restore itself to its last known valid block in case its network is attacked. See figure 11.

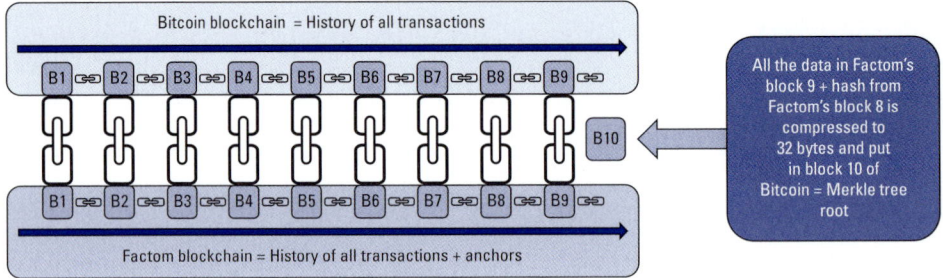

Figure 12   Stabilizing hybrid and private blockchains.

1.2   Summary

You have covered a lot of ground in this chapter. You have learned what a blockchain is and how it is used to secure information. You have discovered the three main types of blockchain networks: public, private and hybrids. You have learned about cryptocurrency and why it is created by public blockchain networks to secure themselves. This chapter has also looked into the differences between cryptocurrency and tokens and how tokens are being used.

This chapter is important as it lays a framework for the rest of the information in this book. After reading it you are prepared for later sections. You are able to talk more confidently about the technology.

1.3   Test your knowledge

1. **What is a blockchain?**
    A. A blockchain is a node time stamper that holds a record of all transactions that have ever occurred on that network.
    B. A blockchain is a time-stamp server that holds a record of all transactions that have ever occurred on that network.
    C. A blockchain is a peer-to-peer distributed time-stamp server that holds a record of all transactions that have ever occurred on that network.
    D. A blockchain is a peer-to-peer distributed time-stamp server that holds some of the records of the blockchain.

2. **What is a hash function in the context of a blockchain?**
   A. A hash function is a mathematical problem that creates an output called a string. These are numbers and letters of any size; for Bitcoin it is 72 bytes.
   B. A hash function adds blocks to the blockchain. And it is the output of a mathematical process that creates a string of numbers and letters of a fixed-size; for Hyperledger it is 32 bytes.
   C. A hash function is used to open up all the data in a block. A hash is the output of this mathematical process that creates a string of numbers and letters of a fixed-size; for Bitcoin it is 82 bytes.
   D. A hash function is used to secure all the data in a block of transactions. A hash is the output of this mathematical process that creates a string of numbers and letters of a fixed-size; for Bitcoin it is 32 bytes.

3. **What is a node?**
   A. A node is a computer that is connected to a blockchain network. It runs the software for the network and keeps the network healthy by transferring information across the network to other nodes.
   B. A node is connected to a blockchain network through the internet. It lets you buy bitcoin.
   C. Nodes are special computers that build blocks. They keep the network running by storing information.
   D. A node transfers information across the network to other nodes.

4. **What is the three-phase process for Fabric?**
   A. One -write a smart contract, two - the endorsed transactions are collected, three - the new block is broadcast back to every peer.
   B. One - an update to the ledger is requested, two - the new block is broadcast back to every peer.
   C. One - an update to the ledger is requested, two - the endorsed transactions are collected, three - the new block is broadcast back to every peer.
   D. One - an update to the ledger is requested, two - the endorsed transactions are collected, three - the node records the transaction in its ledger.

5. **What is a public blockchain network?**
   A. A public blockchain allows some people to participate at any level they want. All have some form of mining and a token.
   B. A public blockchain allows anyone to participate if they identify themselves first. All have some form of mining and a native cryptocurrency.
   C. A public blockchain allows anyone to participate at any level they want. None of them have mining or a native cryptocurrency.
   D. A public blockchain allows anyone to participate at any level they want. All have some form of mining and a native cryptocurrency.

6. **What is a permissioned blockchain network?**
   A. A permissioned blockchain is an open network that utilizes all blockchain technology. Most have mining and no native cryptocurrency.
   B. A permissioned blockchain is a private network that utilizes some blockchain technology including mining for cryptocurrency.
   C. A permissioned blockchain is a closed network that is run on one server. They utilize some blockchain technology but not all. Most don't have mining or any native tokens.
   D. A permissioned blockchain is a private network that utilizes some blockchain technology but not all. Most don't have mining or any native cryptocurrency.

7. **What is a hybrid blockchain network?**
   A. A hybrid network gates full access to its blockchain network. Many have some form of mining and a native cryptocurrency.
   B. A hybrid network does not gate access to its blockchain network. Many don't have any form of mining or a native cryptocurrency.
   C. A hybrid network gates full access to its cryptocurrency. Many have some form of mining and a native cryptocurrency.
   D. A hybrid network is not a blockchain network. Many have some form of mining and a native cryptocurrency.

8. **What is a federated blockchain network?**
   A. A federated blockchain can't be a public blockchain. Users of the system elect nodes to process transactions.
   B. A federated blockchain can be a public blockchain or a private blockchain. Users of the system elect nodes to process transactions.
   C. A federated blockchain is always a public blockchain. Users of the system elect nodes to process transactions.
   D. A federated blockchain allows users of the system to elect nodes to process transactions.

9. **What causes price volatility of cryptocurrencies?**
   A. Cryptocurrency price is driven up and down only by government sanctions.
   B. Cryptocurrency price is driven up and down only by pump and dump scams.
   C. Cryptocurrency price is driven up and down by speculation, scarcity and utility.
   D. Cryptocurrency price is driven up and down only by utility.

10. **How are Merkel tree roots used to stabilize hybrid blockchains?**
    A. Merkle tree root is a type of hardware manufacturer who builds mining chips.
    B. Merkle tree root allows everyone to view information that was published.
    C. Merkle tree root allows the Bitcoin blockchain to restore itself to its last known valid block in case the network is attacked.
    D. Merkle tree root allows a hybrid blockchain to restore itself to its last known valid block in case the network is attacked.

2 Key parts of blockchain technology

Blockchain is a combination of old technologies that have been structured in a new way. In this chapter you will learn more about the key technologies that are used to create a blockchain and the network that supports it. This will include cryptography, ledgers and public witness.

Cryptography is a crucial part of blockchain technology and has been around in one form or another for a very long time. The first known encoded messages occurred in Egypt and Mesopotamia over 3,000 years ago. You will learn about this in depth in the following sections, including how chains are created, what a cryptographic hash is and how encryption works.
In the following sections you will discover how blockchains are created and how the information is secured within them.

You will discover how blockchains use economic incentives to develop resilient public witnesses that adhere to an agreed-upon ruleset. These are the concepts of mining and cryptocurrency that spread the blockchain data across a network.

2.1 Cryptography

Cryptography is the encryption of data so that it is only known by the intended parties. It is one of the most important human inventions and has a very long history. Ancient Greeks and Romans used to send secret messages by substituting letters only decipherable with a secret key.

During World War II innovation in encryption was pushed to new heights, because messages concerning vital information such as troop movements were broadcast. Anyone with a radio could listen to them, and so it was vital that only the intended audience could understand the messages. The Germans developed an encryption machine called Enigma especially designed for the German military (including the navy) so they could send messages over the radio. Later sciences developed a new method that allowed anyone to send each other private and secure messages. In this section you will uncover how encryption works and how we use it today to send secure messages and secure blockchain data.

Machines that encrypted data in the past
The Enigma device was revolutionary. It changed each letter in a complex manner. One letter would swap for another letter multiple times via mechanical rotors. The number of rotors added to the difficulty of the encryption. Only someone with a daily encryption sheet that had the key would know how to unwrap the letters.

Enigma was the strongest encryption method at the time. Eventually, allied forces uncovered how the Germans were encrypting their messages. Joan Clarke and Alan Turing were important code breakers. They would decode messages every day, but this was tremendously difficult.

The Germans kept adding new rotors that would swap the letters more times. Each new rotor added to the mathematical difficulty and eventually made it nearly impossible for Joan Clarke and Alan Turing to solve the encryption key for that day.

The need to solve the German's encryption key led to the development of a mechanical computer called The Bombe. With help from Polish code breakers, Alan Turing developed it at a British government security facility called Bletchley Park. The Bombe could quickly solve the encryption key that was being used by the Germans that day. The Enigma, like all other encryption before, was using what is known as symmetric key encryption. The same key was used to encode a message and decode it.

Modern encryption

The next big leap in encryption did not come until 1975 when Whitfield Diffie and Martin E. Hellman wrote a paper called "New Directions in Cryptography". In it they described a brand-new way of encoding messages. It allowed anyone to send a secret message to another person they had not had contact with before, even without the recipient's encryption key.

If you remember from Enigma, the encryption key was needed both to encode and decode a message. The encryption technique that Diffie and Hellman developed is commonly known as public-key cryptography or more technically "asymmetric cryptography". It uses a pair of keys, both a public key that everyone knows so they can send you an encoded message and a private key only you know so only you can decode messages sent to you.

Asymmetric cryptography allowed, for the first time, anyone to encrypt a message using the recipient's public key, whilst the encrypted message could only be read with the recipient's private key. Private secure communication that we now enjoy on the internet and our phones is all possible thanks to asymmetric cryptography. It is one of the essential technologies that allows blockchain technology to exist. It also allows cryptocurrency to be sent securely from one address to another.

Private and public keys

Let's take a look at how blockchains use asymmetric encryption, known as public-key cryptography, to secure the transfer of cryptocurrency from one address to another.

Blockchain ledgers are widely distributed public accounts that let anyone see who has what cryptocurrency and the full history of that coin over time. Meaning you can look up any transaction and see who sent it.

Asymmetric encryption allows a sender to transfer cryptocurrency to the recipient without someone else being able to steal it. It allows them to do this without having met or exchanged information. As long as the sender has the public key of the recipient, they can send them cryptocurrency.

The public-key on a blockchain is the "address". The address and the private key are connected mathematically and have specific fascinating mathematical properties. The public key and private key are created together by combining randomly chosen, ridiculously huge prime numbers. Prime numbers are whole numbers that can only be divided by themselves.

If you encode a message, such as the transfer of cryptocurrency to a new address, using a recipient's public key, the recipient can decode it using their matching private key and gain ownership of the cryptocurrency. Whoever is in possession of the private key can transfer cryptocurrency to a new address. The ledger holds a record of all these transfers between addresses. Anyone can see the history of transmission between addresses.

The extraordinary mathematical properties of private and public keys make them inverse. If you encrypt a message, such as the transfer of cryptocurrency with your private key, it can only be decrypted by its matching public key. So, when you send a cryptocurrency to a new public address, only the recipient can decode it, and everyone can see that you had the right to transfer cryptocurrency. This is because mathematically only you, with your private key, could have encrypted the transaction. This is called "signing your transaction".

It is evident that you need to keep your private key safe and secure. If your private key is destroyed or lost, you won't be able to transfer your cryptocurrency. If a criminal person copies your private key by physical access to your computer or through malware on your device, then they can transfer your cryptocurrency to a new address. The blockchain will not know that the criminal is pretending to be you and sign your transaction. The transfer of cryptocurrency can only be done with a private key for the public address that the cryptocurrency was last sent to, so once a cryptocurrency has been sent the transaction is irreversible.

2.2 What is a hash?

You have learned how blockchains allow any two parties to send each other cryptocurrency using public and private keys. Sending the cryptocurrency between addresses created transaction receipts. These receipts are written in an ever-expanding record. The record is known as the *blockchain ledger*.

In this section, you will discover how the network secures the records of transfer of cryptocurrency from one address to another using what is known as *hashes*. You should note that this process was pioneered for the transfer of cryptocurrency but can be applied to many other applications where authentication is required. These digital fingerprints of data make sure that the record of ownership is not falsified. Hashes, like most of the technology that makes blockchains, came from a much earlier time. Hans Peter Luhn, an engineer at IBM, first conceived of hashes in the 1950's as a way to organize both numbers and text.

From blocks to hashes

The way that blockchains ensure their records are not corrupted is by using hashes. A hash is similar to symmetric encryption, except that instead of having a key that unlocks the data, the data itself creates a fixed length key via a one-way mathematical proof. The data is the key.

A hashing algorithm is used to take a data input of any size and produce a fixed length string. The fixed length string is the hash and acts as a "signature" or "fingerprint" for the data input. If any of the input data is changed, it will create a completely new digital fingerprint, or rather hash, as can be seen in figure 12.

In the case of blockchains, the data input is a block of transactions.

Each block is run through a hashing algorithm to produce a unique hash that only that block could produce. This unique hash is represented by a fixed length string of numbers and letters. Bitcoin, for example, used a hashing algorithm called SHA256 (Secure Hashing Algorithm 256).

What this means is that all the data in the block can only ever create one unique fixed-length string of numbers and letters. If any of the data in the block is changed or missing, then it would create an entirely different hash. This allows the nodes that are securing the blockchain records to quickly check that everything is intact and has not changed.

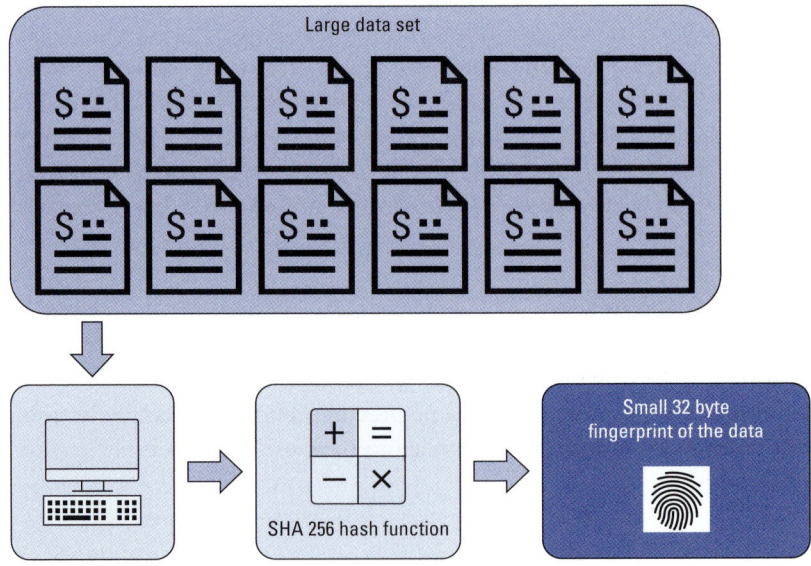

Figure 13   Hashes.

The hashes of each block are published in the next consecutive block creating a chain of records. The hashes prove the order of the blocks and, by default, the order of the transfer of cryptocurrency from one address to another.

Here are some key features of hashes:
- All hashes are deterministic, no matter how many times a block is run through a hash function you will always get the same result.
- Hashes are easy for nodes to compute. Think of this like Sudoku. It is easy to see that the puzzle was solved correctly, but it is difficult to reproduce.
- Hashes must be very sensitive to changes in data input. Any change to the blockchain record will create a completely different hash.
- Hashes must be what is known as "collision resistant". This means that it is practically impossible to create the same hash from two different sets of data.

2.3 Ledgers

Ledgers, the records of economic transactions, are even older technology than encryption. Savvy business owners and governments understood that they needed to account for the things they purchased, orders they had given to traders, and the receipts for these goods later.

Many of the ancient clay tablets from Mesopotamia are accounting logs, known as ledgers, that are over 5,000 years old. The very earliest accounting record known is a 20,000-year-old bone from the Democratic Republic of Congo. It has matched tally marks that were used to account for something. Believe it or not, accounting for things may have been why humans created written languages and mathematics. Ledgers made trade and life in a complex society possible.

Transactions and trade

A transaction is when two parties exchange something. Humans have been looking for better and safer ways to transact with one another since the birth of trade. When our ancestors wanted something that someone else had, they had to be in possession of something their counterparty needed.

For example, if they have some apples, and the other party has some fish then they may have been able to trade some of their apples for the other party's fish. But that did not always work. As I'm sure, you can imagine this type of trade was difficult as the two parties had to have something the other wanted at the same moment. Human ingenuity in trying to solve this difficult trade and transaction problem led to the creation of money.

The birth of money

The first forms of money were goods that everyone wanted all the time and did not deteriorate over time like apples and fish. They were products like salt and beautiful shells. Thousands of years ago Greek slave traders often bartered salt for slaves. And you can still see remnants of these early transactions and money terminology. Expressions like "they are not worth their salt" and the word slave both come from this time. Salt is still used as money by nomads in Africa today.

The next big evolution in terms of money was trusting a third party to hold your funds and protect it from thieves. The Knights Templar were a famous group that set up a network of banks. Their system allowed pilgrims to deposit assets in their home countries and withdraw funds in the Holy Land.

It is believed that they used cryptography to ensure that no one cheated on the amount of funds they would request in their new location. Since the days of the Knights Templar, even more, elaborate schemes have been developed to protect people's assets. The transfer of value is a vulnerable time for disintermediation and holding value of any kind leaves you open to theft.

Trading promises

The notes that were used by pilgrims have evolved significantly. The note itself represented the option to retrieve value. Whoever held the note was in effect the owner of the deposited value that the third party promised to keep safe. This is known as a bearer instrument.

Soon people figured out that they could directly trade notes for goods and services. The abstraction came because both parties agreed that the third party holding the funds was good for the promise and that the note represented a way for the holder to get the gold or silver that it represented if they wished.

Money took another big leap when the United States in 1973 officially ended the gold standard. Many other industrialized nations did as well. Instead of banks holding a tangible asset like gold or silver, they facilitated an intangible asset.

The intangible asset that modern money represents is the future work of people. Each currency is tied to the forthcoming production of a nation or coalition of countries like the EU. This means that currencies no longer have a fixed rate of exchange for gold. Our modern system of banking has floating rates that reflect public sentiment, war and trade agreements.

The idea of money has taken another exciting twist. Some countries like Switzerland and Australia recognize cryptocurrency as a currency. When you distill down why cryptocurrencies have value, it is because they can be provably be exchanged from one individual to another. The blockchain secures the proof of exchange, and the blockchain's consensus algorithm enforces the transfer rules. Cryptocurrencies are not backed by gold or the future output of a country like other currencies. Owning cryptocurrency means that you are in possession of a private key that allows you to send it to another public address.

2.4 The public witness

Another old human concept blockchain technology utilizes is the "public witness". This is possibly the oldest "technology" humans created. A public witness is a person that is attesting to a fact or event. Their testimony allows others to believe that something took place. A witness is spreading their personal knowledge, so more people know and believe it.

The first public witness may have occurred around an ancient campfire as a hunter retold an epic battle to their friends and family. You can see the evidence of these stories painted on the walls of caves across the world. Telling stories and sharing information is deeply human.

A public witness serves two main functions. It spreads knowledge to more than one individual and allows history to become persistent. The more people who know a story, the more persistent it becomes.

The second purpose that a public witness provides is that it allows the individual to make a choice about the information they have been given. Each individual's social norms influence that choice, for example, do they remember the history, do they pass on the information to more people, or do they take action?

In the rest of this section, you will discover how blockchain structures mirror the public witness format. You will learn about the incentive system and the economics that drive the spread of information and the persistence of that information over time.

Computers that witness

Since their creation computers have been developed to do the work that once was only possible by the human mind. They have allowed us to replace countless numbers of once highly paid and skilled workers, such as the code breakers from World War II. Now networks of computers are doing what was only possible through groups of humans working cooperatively. Blockchain technology is an extension of the public witness concept in that it spreads knowledge, encourages persistence of information, and allows each individual node to make a choice with the information that they are given.

Each node on a blockchain network is witnessing information. It is attesting to its accuracy and truthfulness at a later date, much like how court houses, libraries and archives are places where people store information to reference at another point in time. Blockchains are in essence a digital archive.

Each node holds an independent archive of all the transactions that have occurred on its blockchain network. A node hears a "history" and then "chooses" what to do based on the rules of that blockchain.

Every blockchain creates standard rules for how to treat new information. The majority of nodes agree to these rules and operate under them, but each node has a choice and sometimes nodes break the rules or disagree. When only a few nodes disagree on the history of a blockchain, they are ignored.

However, when a large enough group of nodes no longer agree to the same rules, they will break off and start an independent blockchain. This is called a "hardfork". Hardforking means there has been a radical modification to the protocol. The protocol is the set of rules that the majority of nodes agree to follow. Hardforks can make previously invalid blocks or transactions valid. This means that hardforks can, in effect, reverse transactions by changing the rules and rewriting the history of that blockchain.

All nodes and users have to upgrade to the latest version of the protocol software in order to process new transactions and to know what was agreed on the state of the blockchain history. This is important because the history lets you know who has what cryptocurrency.

Much of the fighting in the blockchain community came about because of differences of opinion between what rules should govern the network. These disputes have spawned countless new blockchains, and most are hardforks of Bitcoin.

Mining

Traditional currencies that are controlled by governments such as the US dollar, the Euro and the Yuan are created and distributed by central banks. Each country has a central bank that has the right to issue new money. Often it is done to improve or stimulate their economy. The central bank's job is to keep a country's money supply in balance, so the economy for that country is strong and competitive.

Cryptocurrency is very different. The algorithm, or rather the rules that govern the blockchain, are in charge of the creation of new cryptocurrency. The algorithm facilitates the role of a central bank by either rewarding miners with new cryptocurrency or restricting the issuance of new coins when the competition is high.

Mining does three main things:
- Creating new cryptocurrency;
- Confirming transactions;
- Securing the blockchain history.

Creating new cryptocurrency

The rate at which new cryptocurrency is created and rewarded to miners is set in the rules that govern that blockchain. Each blockchain has unique rules around how often and who can be rewarded.

It is challenging and almost impossible for miners to cheat the system or create a cryptocurrency out of thin air as fake coins are easily recognized. Fake coins will not have a history that matches the blockchain. Miners have to use their computing power and electricity to generate new cryptocurrency like bitcoins.

The creation of new coins is regulated by an algorithm which adjusts the difficulty of the problem that the mining nodes are attempting to solve. The issuance of new coins is dependent on how quickly blocks are solved within a specific timeframe by miners. The difficulty rises and falls because the blockchain's algorithm is making sure it is not too easy or too difficult for miners to gain new bitcoins.

Confirm transactions

Miners play a very important role in the processing and confirmation of transactions. A transaction is when you send a cryptocurrency from one address to another and confirmation occurs for your transaction when a miner includes your transaction in the block they are making. Your transaction is only secure and complete once it has been included in a block.

Securing the blockchain

Miners secure their blockchain network by making it difficult for corrupt individuals to attack, modify or stop the network from functioning. The more miners who operate the system, the more secure the blockchain is considered. This is because the more independent nodes that are physically distant from each other, the more challenging it is to compromise them. An attacker would need to gain control of over 51% of the network before they could do any real damage. Distribution and independence keep blockchains secure and safe.

A 51% attack allows a bad actor to spend the same coins multiple times and to stop the transactions of other users.

The reason this type of attack is not more common is that there is a high monetary cost. The attacker would need to own enough equipment and burn enough electricity to overcome all the other mining nodes on the network. When there are not enough nodes a 51% attack becomes much easier and if that blockchain's cryptocurrency is trading at a higher price than what it would cost to overcome the network, then it is simply a matter of time before the blockchain will be compromised.

Mining's drive to efficiency

Bitcoin miners must always improve the efficiency of the equipment they are using. They are fighting a constant battle to lower the cost of power their equipment consumes to generate new bitcoins. Miners are fighting a never-ending battle of speed, since in order to stay competitive in the network they need to have the fastest machines.

Since Bitcoin's release in 2009, mining hardware has evolved quickly as those with the most efficient equipment will gain a majority of the bitcoins at the lowest cost. It used to be possible to mine using your computer's CPUs or graphic cards. However, the competition for new bitcoins has now become so intense, that in order to have a chance at winning any bitcoin, you will need specialized equipment. The computers that mine bitcoin currently use ASICs chips (Application-Specific Integrated Circuit). ASIC mining chips and the hardware architecture are under continuous pressure to develop. Because electricity is traveling across a switch within the chip, the smaller the distance the faster the chip. When you stack ASICs closer together, they get even faster. With this in mind, bitcoin mining with Yifu Guo's Avalon was 128 nm in 2013, whilst currently ASICs are being taped out for BTC mining closer to the 7nm. New chips become obsolete almost immediately as new faster chips are created, but the promise of easy and lucrative rewards keeps people buying and upgrading their equipment.

Equipment becomes obsolete quickly for two main reasons. The blockchain itself has rules that increase the difficulty of mining if more computers enter the network. These rules act as a stabilizing force and help protect the integrity of the blockchain history.

Mining cryptocurrency is a cannibalistic arms race. In order to obtain the most cryptocurrency miners need to have the most efficient mining operations. Miners with the newest equipment and cheapest electricity win the most blocks. However, the consensus algorithms for each blockchain are striving to maintain a constant rate of transaction clearing and generation of its cryptocurrency. The consensus algorithms adjust the difficulty rate to match the hash power generated by the miners. The more efficient the miners become, the more difficult the blockchain algorithms become.

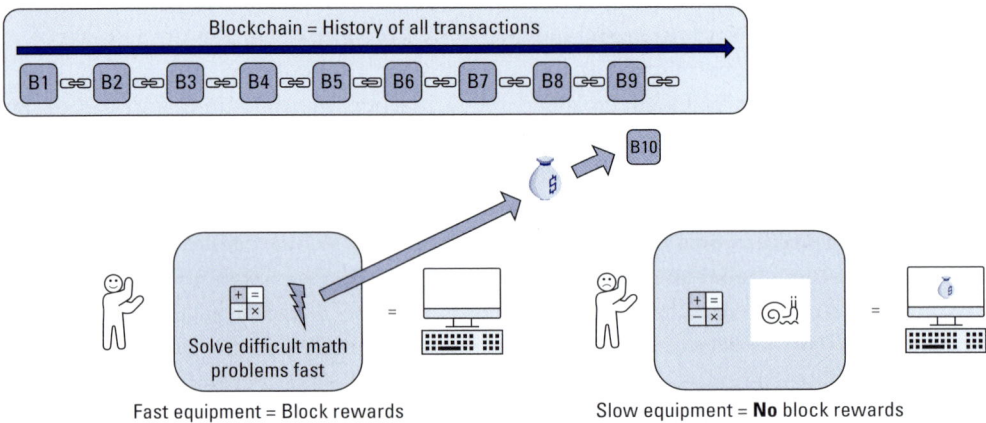

Figure 14   The fastest nodes win cryptocurrency.

New distributed network structures

Blockchains are distributed ledgers. They create a nearly unchangeable history of transaction records that are maintained by a decentralized network. All records secured in the blockchain have been approved by an agreed-on rule set called consensus. But not all distributed ledgers are blockchains.

The very public nature of blockchain technology and structure has gained the attention of most governments, banks and businesses. The security that the system offers and the ability to confidently transact with a counterparty directly is fascinating. Many institutions are exploring blockchain technology to create improvements and efficiency in their operations.

But the very public nature of their records is off putting. Many institutions need to keep their records private for a variety of reasons. And because blockchains are often subject to attack and down times that would crash an economy if everyone switched to using a blockchain system, it is unappealing for a country's critical systems such as to operate based upon blockchain without complete assurance. Large institutions have been picking apart the elements of blockchain they like best. Many institutions see the benefit of having a shared distributed ledger.

Distributed ledger technology, or DLT as it is often called, is a network of known parties collaborating in the creation and balances of a shared record. DLT does not have miners, because everyone who has the ledger and the ability to edit has incentives to maintain its integrity. Because DLT has no mining, it has no cryptocurrency. But oddly enough it can be used to issue a token that can operate like a cryptocurrency.

DLT networks are not decentralized. Whoever creates a distributed ledger has complete control. They manage the structure, purpose and how the network functions. In normal practice there is more than one instance of a ledger's history stored across many servers, and more than one node works to update and confirm new information. The nodes will communicate with one another to ensure that the most accurate and up-to-date record of transactions is maintained. These types of networks rely on similar principles of consensus just like traditional blockchains. They have rules that help ensure all the nodes are acting correctly, which is important even when all the parties are known.

2.5 Summary

In this chapter, you learned more about the history and evolution of technology that led to the creation of blockchains and cryptocurrencies. This chapter has explored the slow evolution of encryption, from the early Roman techniques to the revolution of public-key encryption that allowed for modern conveniences such as email. You discovered how hashes are created and the purpose they serve in blockchain technology.

This chapter is fundamental as it uncovers the core technologies that are used to create a blockchain. Having an understanding of how these different technologies work and are used demystifies blockchain technology. It reveals its limitations and vulnerabilities.

After reading this chapter you will be better prepared to lead projects that look to utilize blockchain technology. Your understanding of the limitations and the core functions of the different parts of a blockchain will enable you to make more informed choices when choosing technology and designing your systems.

2.6 Test your knowledge

1. **What is cryptography?**
   A. Cryptography is the encryption of data so that it is only known by the intended parties.
   B. Cryptography is the mixing of data so that it is only known by you.
   C. Cryptography is the publishing of data so that it is readable by everyone.
   D. Cryptography is a type of mathematics.

2. **What is the Enigma device?**
   A. The Enigma device was invented by the English to confuse the Germans during WWII.
   B. The Enigma device was a computer that changed letters in a message in a complex manner.
   C. The Enigma device was a mechanical cryptography device that changed radio channels.
   D. The Enigma device was a mechanical cryptography device that changed letters in a message in a complex manner.

3. **What is public-key encryption?**
   A. It uses an asymmetric pair of keys that everyone knows. When you receive a message, you decode it with your key.
   B. It uses asymmetric cryptography to allow you to send messages across private channels while keeping the content private.
   C. It uses asymmetric cryptography to allow you to send messages across public channels while keeping the content private. It uses a pair of keys, both a public key that everyone knows and a private key only you know. When you receive a message, you decode it with your private key.
   D. It uses symmetric cryptography to allow you to send messages across public channels while keeping the content private. It uses a pair of keys, both a public key that everyone knows and a private key only you know.

4. **What is a private key?**
   A. A private key lets you encode messages sent to you over public channels.
   B. A private key lets you decode messages sent to you over public channels.
   C. A private key lets you enter public channels.
   D. A private key lets you publish information on public channels.

5. **What is a public key?**
   A. A public key allows anyone to send you a private message over a public channel.
   B. A public key lets you decode messages.
   C. A public key opens up a public channel.
   D. A public key allows known people to send you a private message over a public channel.

6. **What is a hash?**
   A. A hash is a two-way mathematical proof of data. It creates a digital fingerprint of information and allows you to take a data input of any size and produce a fixed-length string.
   B. A hash is a three-way mathematical proof of data. It creates a large data file of information.
   C. A hash is a one-way mathematical proof of data. It creates a digital fingerprint of information and allows you to take a data input of any size and produces a fixed-length string.
   D. A hash is a one-way mathematical proof of data. It creates a large data file of information.

7. **Do you always get the same fixed-length string from a data set when it is hashed?**
   A. Yes, hashes are deterministic, no matter how many times a block runs through a hash function, you will always get the same result.
   B. No, hashes are always unique.
   C. Hashes will always give two results.
   D. Hashes can be decrypted with a private key.

8. **What is a ledger?**
   A. A ledger is a record of bitcoins.
   B. A ledger is a tool for encryption.
   C. A ledger is a record of economic transactions.
   D. A ledger is device to store bitcoin.

9. **In the context of blockchains, what is a "public witness"?**
   A. A node on a blockchain network is a public witness. It is attesting to the accuracy and truthfulness of information.
   B. A witness that attests to its accuracy and truthfulness of information.
   C. A digital court house, library, or archive where people store information to reference.
   D. A person sending a transaction over a public network.

10. **Mining on a blockchain does what three things?**
    A. Mining hides cryptocurrency, broadcasts transactions and publishes a history of transactions.
    B. Mining creates new cryptocurrency, confirms transactions and secures the blockchain's history.
    C. Mining creates new cryptocurrency, blocks bad transactions and secures the blockchain's history.
    D. Mining creates tokens, confirms assets and secures the blockchain's history.

3 The structure of the network: consensus algorithm

A consensus algorithm is a code that governs how a blockchain operates. It sets the rules that all participants must follow to process transactions. Consensus algorithms create a network structure and process that allows a group of independent systems to agree on a single version of the truth. Consensus algorithms are not unique to blockchain technology, but they are the foundation of all blockchains. They are the set of rules that govern how each blockchain functions.

It is essential to understand the different common blockchain network structures and the consensus algorithms that dictate their structure. Understanding these structures will empower you to make informed design decisions when building applications and processing transactions.
In this section, you will uncover many of the most significant consensus rules that govern how blockchains work. You will discover how these algorithms impact the functionality and, by extension, the best use you can obtain from blockchains that utilize this type of consensus algorithm.

3.1 Proof of Work

Proof of Work (PoW) was proposed by Satoshi Nakamoto and is still used by Bitcoin, Ethereum, Litecoin, Dogecoin and many other public blockchains. It is a competitive consensus algorithm where each mining node on the blockchain is competing to secure blocks. It allows anyone to participate at any level in the creation and maintenance of the system but is very competitive. Nodes that hope to be competitive and be rewarded with cryptocurrency will need to operate specialized equipment. The algorithm is, by design, energy intensive and expensive. The expense and difficulty of obtaining bitcoins was an intentional part of the token economics. Much like mining gold, it is not cheap nor easy to mine, and the difficulty and scarcity of bitcoins is thought to drive part of the value of the asset.

The Proof of Work algorithm functions by having some of the participants of the Bitcoin blockchain, called miners, solve a complex computational problem. The miner who solves the problem first adds a new block of transactions to Bitcoin's blockchain. The miner is then given a "block reward" with bitcoins. Currently, miners receive 12.5 bitcoins for finishing first. The number of bitcoins rewarded to miners decreases over time.

The number of miners competing for bitcoins changes frequently because each miner is participating willingly and freely. The Proof of Work algorithm will adjust the difficulty of the problem the miners are solving in order to maintain a more consistent time between blocks and to ensure the security of the transactions that are being secured in each block.

It is not uncommon for more than one miner to solve a block problem concurrently. When this happens, miners pick one of the wining blocks to continue building their chain. The longest chain wins. It is recommended that you wait for at least six blocks before confirming a transaction. You do this to ensure that enough blocks have been secured on top of the block your transaction was placed within.

The Bitcoin blockchain is protected from corruption as long as 51% or more of the blocks being created by miners are legitimate. The miners are economically incentivized only to produce valid blocks.

PoW tends to be used for peer-to-peer transaction between parties that are not connected. It can be expensive to scale applications that are built within PoW blockchains (Decentralized application, DApp) as they can be expensive and cumbersome to operate.

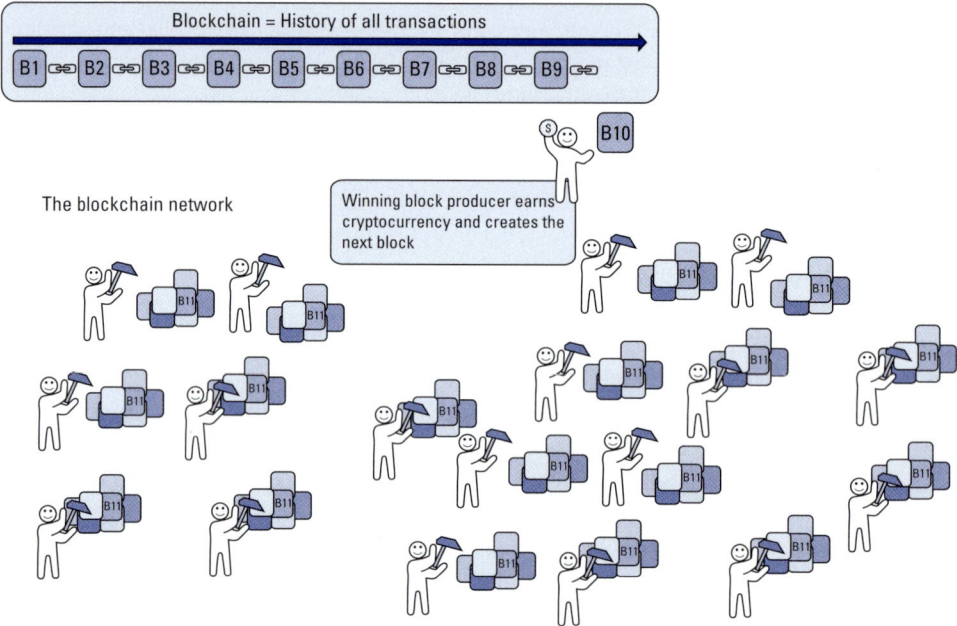

Figure 15   Proof of Work.

Pros:
- It has been tested since 2009 and still works great;
- It is slower and safer - you know your transaction will not be rolled back;
- It is trustless - no one can block your transaction from processing.

Cons:
- It's slow - you have to wait for your transaction to be confirmed;
- It's costly - transaction costs can go up with the number of users;
- It's susceptible to centralization over time - those with the most recourses can pool together their efforts in mining.

3.2   Proof of Stake (PoS)

Proof of Stake (PoS) is a competitive consensus algorithm. It was created as an alternative to the Proof of Work (PoW) because blockchains had difficulty meeting the transaction speed demands.

PoS nodes do not mine cryptocurrency. Users can put some of their cryptocurrency, from a blockchain, in a retainer. This retainer allows the user to "stake" that they will process transactions honestly and by the rules of the consensus system. If the user fails to do so, they will forfeit their cryptocurrency. It is becoming popular in public blockchain networks as it is a low-cost alternative that supports greater decentralization.

Proof of Stake allows anyone to participate at any level in the creation and maintenance of the network. The one catch is that a node operator must have the minimum amount of cryptocurrency needed to stake. If they do, they can process transactions for the network. The node's probability of securing the next block and being rewarded for doing so is equivalent to the percentage of cryptocurrency they stake.

In the event that there are two or more competing blocks (known as a fork) in the Proof of Stake algorithm, you can stake your cryptocurrency on both blocks without consequence. This is called the "nothing-at-stake" problem. It is important to note that in a Proof of Work system it is not economically viable to mine on both chains. But in PoS, there is little cost involved in working on several chains and an economic incentive to do so. There are open questions regarding what rules would be applied across PoS environments when situations arise where a staker is nefarious from start. See figure 16.

Pros:
- It is energy efficient and does not burn electricity when mining;
- It can be more expensive to attack than PoW - hackers need to purchase a large percentage of the native cryptocurrency;
- It scales easily to handle transaction load and size.

Cons:
- Rewards are weighted to those who stake their cryptocurrency the longest. The longer a miner stakes, the greater the reward. The network structure allows wealthy stakers to control more of the network and this may cause centralization and censorship.

PoS is used by Ethereum, Peercoin and Nxt.

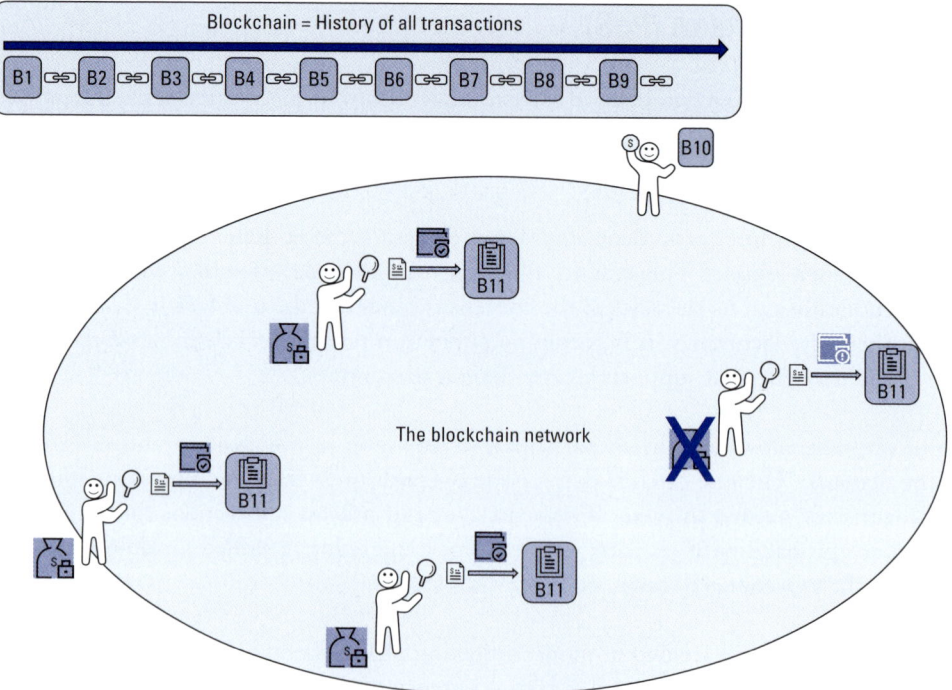

Figure 16   Proof of Stake.

3.3   Delegated Proof of Stake

The competition to be a validator happens outside of consensus. Those with better websites and social media accounts, at this point, are selected. Delegated Proof of Stake (DPoS) is a collaborative effort, and nodes that are validating transactions are rewarded equally in this consensus system.

As a stakeholder you elect "witnesses" who will validate transactions and create blocks for the network. EOS, one of the most popular DPoS blockchains, only has 21 witnesses.

Each of the EOS witnesses are paid fees for producing blocks, and the fee is set by the stakeholders.

The witness nodes produce blocks one at a time in a round-robin fashion, or by random selection. Witnesses can't publish consecutive blocks or execute double-spending attacks where they allow cryptocurrency to be sent twice or more from the same address without updating the ownership. This would be the equivalent to writing checks from an empty bank account that you don't own. The person you wrote the check to believes they have been paid, but once the check is processed by the bank, it is rejected, and they learn that they have been defrauded.

DPoS networks are used to build applications as they allow developers to scale up the size and increase the speed of their products.

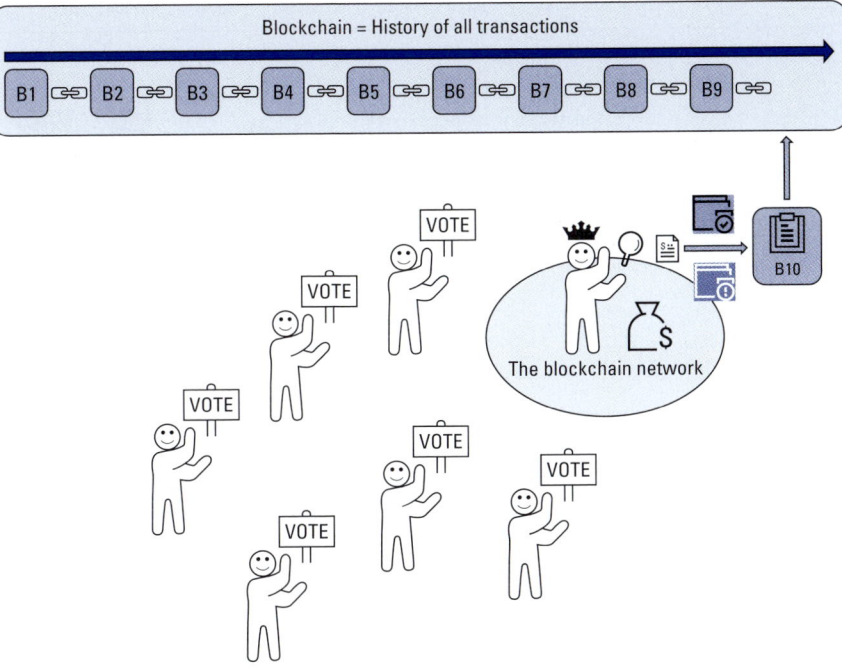

Figure 17   Delegated Proof of Stake.

Pros:
- Like PoS, it is energy efficient;
- It is fast - for example, EOS has a block-time of 0.5 second.

Cons:
- It is a centralized system - this may make it prone to corruption.

3.4 Proof of Authority

Best suited for private, permissioned blockchains, Proof of Authority (PoA) blockchains have a collaborative consensus algorithm. In this system transactions and blocks are validated by approved accounts. The validator nodes run consensus software, allowing them to put transactions in blocks.

This system is best used for test networks that are used to test applications before they are deployed on public networks.

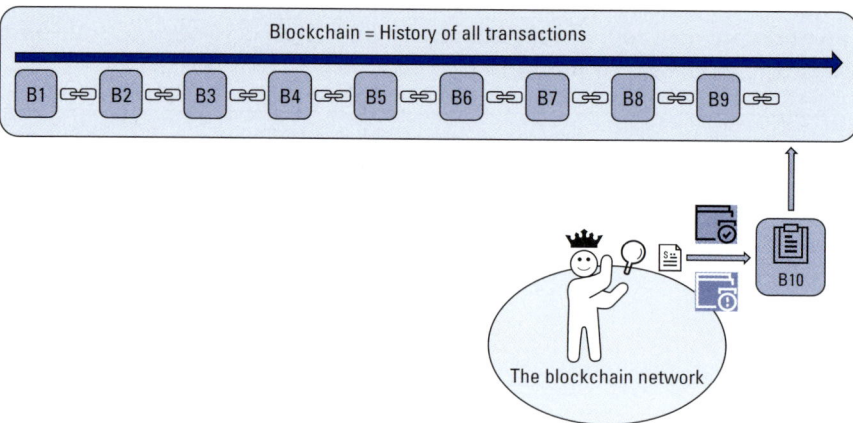

Figure 18   Proof of Authority.

Pros:
- Energy efficient;
- Fast.

Cons:
- Centralized.

PoA is used by PoA Network, Ethereum Kovan test net and VeChain.

3.5 Proof of Elapsed Time

Proof of Elapsed Time (PoET) is a competitive consensus algorithm that is often used by permissioned blockchains to decide the mining rights on the system. If you remember, a permissioned blockchain requires any prospective participant to identify themselves before they are allowed to join. The consensus algorithm was developed for the Sawtooth Lake project on Hyperledger. It was built to run in a secure area of the central processor of your computer, called a trusted execution environment (TEE). PoET leverages the security of the TEE to prove that time has passed by time-stamping each transaction.

PoET has a lottery system that randomly selects a node from the pool of validating nodes. The probability of a node being selected increases in line with how much processing resource that node has contributed to that blockchain.

PoET allows you to control the cost of the consensus process. It is great for internal projects or ones where all the participants are known. It can be used to build decentralized applications.

The structure of the network: consensus algorithm

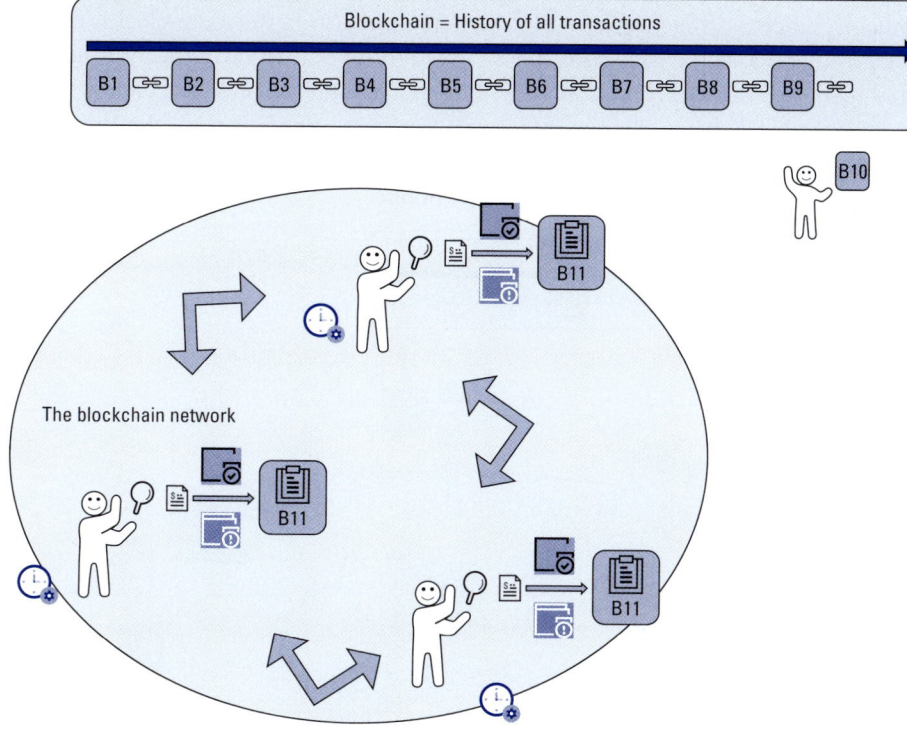

Figure 19   Proof of Elapsed Time.

Pros:
- Low cost of upkeep;
- Scalable to operation.

Cons:
- Needs specialized hardware;
- Must know participants in the network.

PoET is used by Hyperledger - Sawtooth Lake project.

3.6   Proof of Capacity and Proof of Space

Proof-of-Space (PoSpace) and Proof-of-Capacity (PoC) blockchains typically have a collaborative consensus, where nodes that are securing transactions - these can be called "farmers" - allocate a non-trivial amount of their memory or disk space. The great thing about this type of consensus is that almost anyone can become a "farmer" and this allows for greater decentralization of the network. The main difference you should be aware of between Proof of Space and Proof of Work is two-fold. Firstly, instead of using your processing power to compete to secure the blockchain, you use your leftover memory.

The other significant difference is that farmers are not fighting to secure blocks. PoSpace is another green and scalable consensus like POS (Proof of Stake), but instead of needing to own and hold cryptocurrency, you can use resources you already have and are not currently using. PoSpace blockchains may be a fairer and greener alternative to other blockchains. They can be used to build applications and transfer value. However, most of them are new and have yet to undergo rigorous testing by the public.

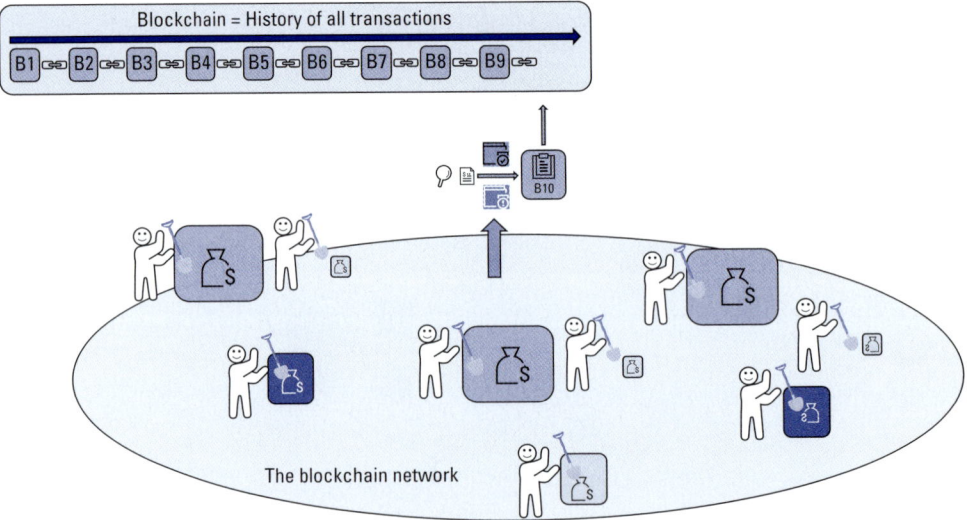

Figure 20   Proof of Capacity and Proof of Space.

Pros:
- Uses wasted hardware space;
- Environmentally friendly.

Cons:
- New and not tested.

PoSpace and PoC are used by Burstcoin, Chia and SpaceMint.

3.7 Proof of Burn

Most "Proof of Burn" systems have a noncompetitive consensus algorithm. Transactions are validated often by elected nodes. These nodes check to see if the fee has been paid. A user pays the fee by "burning" some cryptocurrency. Burning means sending their cryptocurrency to an address where it can never be retrieved. Within the Factom blockchain this action grants the user the ability to publish a transaction. This transaction can be about anything and has been used to secure things like land titles, birth records and data feeds on IoT (Internet of Things) devices. The utility is in the performance of the data and the ability to validate the data publicly.

Each system is a little different, and it is worth discovering how the Proof of Burn is implemented. Miner nodes may burn the native currency or the currency of an alternative chain, like Bitcoin.

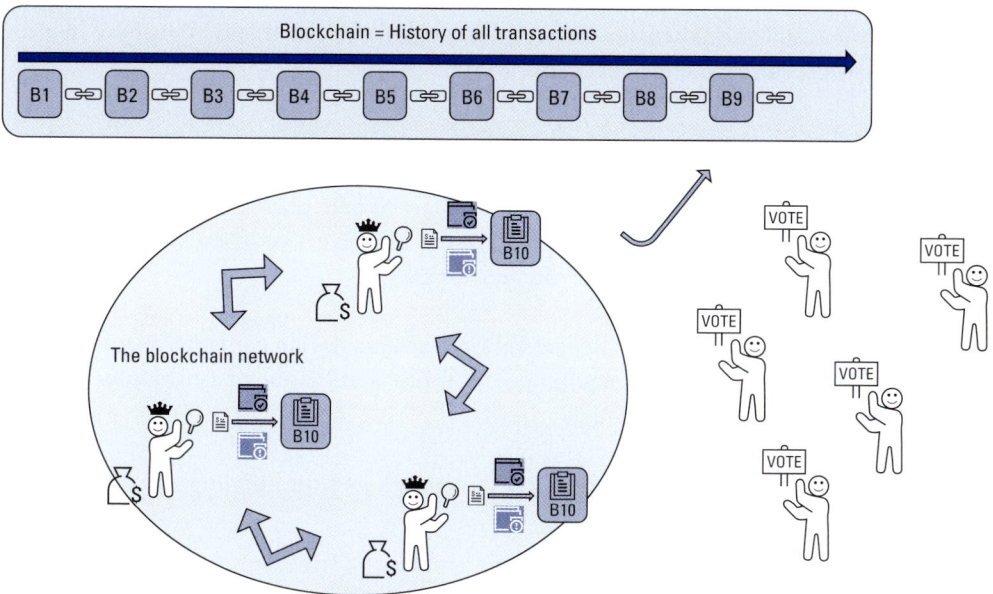

Figure 21   Proof of Burn.

Pros:
- Cheap to use;
- Scalable to all types of applications.

Cons:
- Centralization;
- Limited functionality.

Proof of Burn is used by Slimcoin, TGCoin and Factom.

3.8   Hyperledger Fabric

Hyperledger Fabric's consensus encompasses more than simply agreeing on the order of transactions. It includes the entire transaction flow, from proposal and endorsement through to ordering, validation and commitment. Fabric's consensus is a full-circle verification of the correctness of a set of transactions comprising all blocks.

The Fabric network uses a process where the validating nodes provide a guaranteed ordering of the transaction and check those blocks of transactions that need to be committed to the ledger.

Consensus must ensure:
- Confirmation of the correctness of all transactions;
- Agreement on order and correctness, together with the global state of the blockchain.

You get to consensus only when the order and results of a block's transactions have met the policy and have been thoroughly checked.

Nodes work a little differently, since each application creator can set their own rules around what validation means for their application and who is allowed to validate transactions. The application creators establish when checks and balances take place during the lifecycle of their transactions. Chaincode, Hyperledger's version of a smart contract, is used to ensure and enforce the policies that the application creators set.

It is worth pointing out that a Hyperledger Fabric Node is a docker container that is running Fabric. You don't need specialized equipment, you just need access to a computer in order to create your own network.

Fabric is great for creating a private blockchain network and for building applications that will be used by known parties.

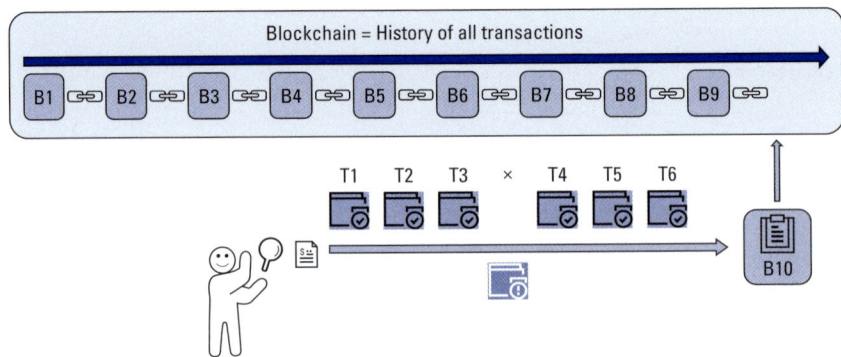

Figure 22   Hyperledger Fabric's consensus.

Pros:
- Cheap to use;
- Scalable to all types of applications.

Cons:
- Completely centralized.

3.9 Summary

Consensus algorithms are not only crucial to the function of each blockchain, they also dictate the network structure. The algorithms determine what makes a valid transaction and who is allowed to mine and secure the network. Every blockchain has a slightly different network structure and this chapter has only covered a few of the dozens of network structures that are currently being tested.

It is essential to understand the different types of consensus algorithms that are out there and how they differ, because they will significantly impact the applications that are built on them. The fundamental infrastructure of any blockchain is its proof mechanism. It is important to understand the features of these proof mechanisms as they relate to the needs in terms of latency, integrity and applicability.

The consensus algorithm can make transactions free but not secure. They may make transactions very secure but too slow to run your application. Understanding these trade-offs will help you make informed decisions on which blockchain is best for the goals that you have.

3.10 Test your knowledge

1. **What is Proof of Work?**
   A. Proof of Work is a competitive consensus algorithm that is common in public blockchain networks. It allows anyone to participate at any level in the creation and maintenance of the system. Nodes that hope to be competitive and be rewarded with cryptocurrency will need to operate specialized equipment.
   B. Proof of Work is a collaborative consensus algorithm that is common in private blockchain networks. It allows anyone to participate at any level in the creation and maintenance of the system. Nodes that hope to be competitive and be rewarded with cryptocurrency will need to operate specialized equipment.
   C. Proof of Work is a competitive consensus and a network structure that supports a large pool of validator nodes. The validator nodes are elected by users of the system. The users pledge funds to the validator of their choice. If a node wins the election, they are granted the right to process transactions.
   D. Proof of Work is a collaborative consensus algorithm that is becoming popular in public blockchain networks. It allows anyone to participate at any level in the creation and maintenance of the network. As long as a node operator has the minimum amount of cryptocurrency needed to stake, they can process transactions for the network.

2. **What is the network structure of a Proof of Work blockchain?**
   A. Proof of Work has a network structure that supports a very small centralized pool of nodes. The nodes collaborate to validate transactions and solve complex mathematical puzzles. The nodes are independent of the transactions they process and are compensated by the network for the work involved in processing transaction by receiving a mining reward and transaction fees.

B. Proof of Work has a network structure that supports interdependent nodes. The nodes pool all of their cryptocurrency and are then granted the right to process transactions in their pool. If they fail to abide by the rules of the network, they are kicked out.
C. Proof of Work has a network structure that supports many structures and is very flexible. Each application creator sets their own rules for validation and who is allowed to validate transactions.
D. Proof of Work has a network structure that supports a large pool of independent nodes. The nodes compete to validate transactions and solve complex mathematical puzzles. The nodes are independent of the transactions they process and are compensated by the network for the work involved in processing transaction by receiving a mining reward and transaction fees.

3. **What is Proof of Stake?**
    A. Proof of Stake is a competitive consensus algorithm that is becoming popular in private blockchain networks. It allows anyone to participate at any level in the creation and maintenance of the network. As long as a node operator has the minimum amount of cryptocurrency needed to stake, they can process transactions for the network.
    B. Proof of Stake is a collaborative consensus algorithm that is becoming popular in public blockchain networks. It allows a select few to participate at any level in the creation and maintenance of the network. As long as a node operator has the minimum amount of cryptocurrency needed to stake, they can process transactions for the network.
    C. Proof of Stake is a competitive consensus algorithm that is becoming popular in public blockchain networks. It allows anyone to participate at any level in the creation and maintenance of the network. As long as a node operator has the minimum amount of cryptocurrency needed to stake, they can process transactions for the network.
    D. Proof of Stake is a collaborative consensus algorithm that is becoming popular in public blockchain networks. It allows anyone to participate at any level in the creation and maintenance of the network. As long as a node operator has the minimum amount of cryptocurrency needed to stake, they can process transactions for the network.

4. **What is the network structure of Proof of Stake?**
    A. Proof of Stake has a network structure that supports interdependent nodes. The nodes pool all of their cryptocurrency and are then granted the right to process transactions in their pool. If they fail to abide by the rules of the network, they are kicked out.
    B. Proof of Stake has a network structure that supports a large pool of independent nodes. The nodes "stake" a pool of cryptocurrency and are then granted the right to process transactions. If they fail to abide by the rules of the network, they will forfeit the cryptocurrency that they have staked.

C. Proof of Stake has a network structure that supports a large pool of independent nodes. The nodes pool their cryptocurrency and are then granted the right to process transactions. If they fail to abide by the rules of the network, they will forfeit the cryptocurrency that they have staked.

D. Proof of Stake has a network structure that supports a few codependent nodes. The nodes "stake" a pool of cryptocurrency and are then granted the right to process transactions. If they fail to abide by the rules of the network, they will forfeit the cryptocurrency that they have staked.

5. **What is Delegated Proof of Stake?**
   A. Delegated Proof of Stake has a network structure that supports a large pool of independent nodes. The nodes compete to validate transactions and solve complex mathematical puzzles. The nodes are independent of the transactions they process and are compensated by the network for the work of processing transaction by receiving a mining reward and transaction fees.
   B. Delegated Proof of Stake is a consensus algorithm that is uncommon in public blockchain networks. It only allows a few dedicated nodes to participate in the creation and maintenance of the network.
   C. Delegated Proof of Stake is a consensus algorithm that is uncommon in public blockchain networks. It only allows thousands of nodes to participate in the creation and maintenance of the network.
   D. Delegated Proof of Stake is a consensus algorithm that is common in public blockchain networks. It only allows a few dedicated nodes to participate in the creation and maintenance of the network.

6. **What is the network structure of Delegated Proof of Stake?**
   A. Delegated Proof of Stake has a network structure that supports a small pool of validator nodes. The validator nodes are randomly selected by the system. The users pledge funds to the validator of their choice.
   B. Delegated Proof of Stake has a network structure that supports a large pool of validator nodes. The validator nodes are elected by users of the system. The users pledge funds to the validator of their choice. If a node wins the election, they are granted the right to process transactions.
   C. Delegated Proof of Stake has a network structure that supports a small pool of validator nodes. The validator nodes are elected by users of the system. The users pledge funds to the validator of their choice. If a node wins the election, they are granted the right to process transactions.
   D. Delegated Proof of Stake supports many structures. Each application creator sets their own rules for validation and who is allowed to validate transactions.

7. **What is Proof of Authority?**
   A. Proof of Authority is a consensus algorithm that is used by test nets. It allows users to simulate a blockchain at little to no cost.
   B. Proof of Authority is a consensus algorithm that is used by governments. It allows users to create a fully distributed blockchain at little to no cost.
   C. Proof of Authority is a consensus algorithm that supports a small pool of validator nodes. The validator nodes are elected by users of the system. The users pledge funds to the validator of their choice. If a node wins the election, they are granted the right to process transactions.
   D. Proof of Authority is a consensus algorithm that uses the secure area of the central processor of a computer, called a trusted execution environment, to prove that time has passed by time-stamping each transaction.

8. **What is Proof of Elapsed Time?**
   A. Proof of Elapsed Time is a consensus algorithm structure that supports a small pool of validator nodes.
   B. Proof of Elapsed Time is a consensus algorithm that is used by test nets. It allows users to simulate a blockchain at a little to no cost.
   C. Proof of Elapsed Time is a consensus algorithm that mines using a node's trusted execution environment to prove that time has passed by time-stamping each block.
   D. Proof of Elapsed Time is a consensus algorithm that uses the secure area of the central processor of a computer, called a trusted execution environment, to prove that time has passed by time-stamping each transaction.

9. **What is Proof of Capacity?**
   A. Proof of Capacity is a competitive consensus algorithm that allows almost anyone to become a "farmer" by utilizing their unused memory.
   B. Proof of Capacity is a consensus algorithm that allows a select few to become a "farmer" by utilizing their unused memory.
   C. Proof of Capacity is a collaborative consensus algorithm that allows almost anyone to become a "farmer" by utilizing their unused memory.
   D. Proof of Capacity is a collaborative consensus algorithm. Almost anyone can mine blocks and win rewards.

10. **What is the network structure of Hyperledger Fabric?**
    A. Hyperledger Fabric supports many structures. Each application creator sets their own rules for validation and who is allowed to validate transactions.
    B. Hyperledger Fabric supports proof of work. Each application creator sets how many nodes will process their transactions.
    C. Hyperledger Fabric supports proof of stake. Each application creator sets their own rules for validation and who is allowed to validate transactions.
    D. Hyperledger Fabric supports many structures. Fabric sets the rules for validation and who is allowed to validate transactions.

4 Key blockchain networks and technologies

The concept of a blockchain network is better understood by first breaking it into two parts: blockchain and network and defining the two separately. A blockchain is a public and widely copied record of all the transactions that have ever occurred on a blockchain. This record is often referred to as a ledger, like what a businessperson would use to keep track of sales and inventory. A ledger within blockchain is a record of events and transactions that have occurred since that blockchain's inception to the present moment. The record is ever growing. As new transactions occur, they are written into the record and replicated, validated and time-stamped.

For example, when you send your friend Mary some bitcoin, that transaction record is entered into the Bitcoin blockchain. The transaction record allows the network to know that the bitcoin that was once assigned to your address has now been assigned to Mary's Bitcoin address.

The record of your transaction is spread across a network of computers that each hold a complete transaction history for Bitcoin. The number of computers varies every moment because each computer referred to as a node is operated independently. Bitcoin normally has 10,000 or more nodes but a blockchain network only needs two.

The more computers that are updating a record of transactions and competing with each other to keep the records up to date, the better.

A simple way to think about blockchain networks is that the more nodes there are, the more secure the network is. But this security comes at a high cost. The trade-off with having more computers, is that the record takes longer to be recorded securely. Another trade-off is the difficulty each computer has in competing within the network. The nodes most burn more electricity to secure the network and that costs money.

Blockchain networks do not have a central server to coordinate and facilitate communication among computers. It is a peer-to-peer network and each node communicates directly with other nodes. All the computers are operating on a shared rule set that lets them know how to update transactions and collaborate with other nodes. An important part of their collaboration is the agreement on the current and past state of the records. They must agree on the validity of transactions. In the example above where you sent your friend Mary some bitcoin, at least 51% of the computers on the Bitcoin network need to agree that your transaction happened. The network's agreement about the history is called consensus.

It is vital that each node has a complete history, so they can determine that the location of each cryptocurrency unit is accurate, and no fraud has occurred. When a new computer joins the system, the first thing it does is to borrow an up-to-date copy from one of the peers.

However, that is not where the magic happens. The magic happens when there is a need to update the ledger, which is always. All copies on the network must synchronize by having a majority of the nodes agree on which transactions to add to the ledger.

Besides recording transactions like the one where you sent your friend Mary some Bitcoin, blockchain networks have grown in their functionality. Each blockchain protocol has been tailored to appeal to different applications. Some networks have increased their speed and reduced the number of nodes they can accommodate so users can have faster confirmation times on transactions. Other networks have expanded their capabilities in order to facilitate things like simple websites, gaming platforms, and smart contracts. These blockchain applications are called decentralized applications (DApp).

The blockchains can store and process the data these applications collect and generate, and work much like the server behind your favorite phone app does. However, there is one important thing to remember: blockchains are designed to store information forever, so they can prove their history. DApps that produce any amount of information and want to store it in their blockchain will run into some high cost.

4.1 The history of blockchain networks

The blockchain network is a product of technologies that have been around for a long time, some thousands of years. The essential components of the blockchain network innovation include cryptography, peer-to-peer networking, proof of work, and digital signatures.

Cryptography has been part of human society since ancient Mesopotamia, Greece, and Egypt, in other words for over 3,000 years. Of course, the specific styles and methods have changed over time. The public-private key or asymmetric cryptography used in most blockchain networks was invented in the 1960s and is widely used in other areas of the internet.

Meanwhile, blind digital signatures were first described by David Chaum in an academic paper he published in 1983. David Chaum is best known for founding Digicash in 1989, a company that launched the first electronic cash. Chaum's double-spend inroads are reflected in all blockchains and he founded Elixxir, a blockchain network that began in 2017.

The Proof of Work (PoW), a critical component in how computers on a peer-to-peer network form consensus on the status of a shared ledger, was first described in an academic paper titled "Pricing via Processing or Combatting Junk Mail", published in 1992. Computer scientists Cynthia Dwork and Moni Naor wrote the paper.

Later in 1997 the British cryptographer Adam Back developed Hashcash, a Proof of Work system that helped to limit email spam. Adam Back is currently a co-founder at Blockstream, a company that brings together many of Bitcoin's core developers to build scaling solutions for blockchain networks.

Meanwhile, peer-to-peer networking has been used since the early days of the internet. The internet itself is a vast peer-to-peer network.

On October 31, 2008, Satoshi Nakamoto published a white paper titled "Bitcoin: A Peer-to-Peer Electronic Cash System" on the Cypherpunk mailing list. Cypherpunk is a forum founded in the late 1980s to advocate the use of technology, including cryptography, to make society more open and free by overcoming the tyranny of government and huge corporations. Some of the active participants in the Cypherpunk movement included David Chaum and Wikileaks founder Julian Assange.

In the white paper, Satoshi Nakamoto describes how the first blockchain network was to work. On January 3, 2009, Satoshi Nakamoto launched Bitcoin, the first blockchain network. It was a completely new service but one whose building blocks have been used for a very long time. Now there are thousands of blockchain networks. Some look very similar to Bitcoin like Litecoin and Bitcoin Cash, while others such as Ethereum, Hyperledger, and EOS are very different and host a vast number of DApps.

Blockchain technology has come a long way. In Deloitte's 2019 Global Blockchain Survey: "Blockchain gets down to business" that interviewed 1,386 senior executives across twelve countries: Brazil, Canada, China, Germany, Hong Kong, Israel, Luxembourg, Singapore, Switzerland, United Arab Emirates, United Kingdom, and the United States, 53% of these executives said that blockchain technology was a critical priority for their company in 2019. Well-designed pilots within many of these companies have shown the value of blockchain's utility and the ability to scale into production.

4.2 Top challenges for blockchain networks

A key issue that has plagued the blockchain industry is the lack of skilled and talented developers needed for the thousands of projects. Given the relative age of the technology and the unique challenges that come with its distribution, finding great talent has been hard. With few excellent developers within the space, many projects have suffered from exuberant ideas and not enough talent to complete them, whilst many have faced security risks and poor design and execution.

One of the primary use cases for blockchain technology has been digital identity and the transfer of value. Banking and consumer identity are highly regulated fields. Regulations have limited innovation in terms of payment and identity software development, and this has been both good and bad.

Blockchains are doing things that have not been achieved or imagined before and the technology may reshape society as much as the internet has over the last 30 years. However, the reaction from some governments has been harsh to protect the status quo from disruption. A few countries have banned cryptocurrencies within their borders. These include China,

Russia, Vietnam, and Bolivia. Other countries have made it hard to trade assets held on blockchain networks.

Another issue that blockchains networks are struggling with is their interoperability with other blockchains. The open source nature of most blockchain development means that there are no organized coordination or standards. Efforts are now being made by many universities to create standards in terminology and best practices in development.

The internet has succeeded because of the collaboration between different stakeholders who have existed since the early days. Bodies like the Internet Corporation for Assigned Names and Numbers (ICANN) and the Internet Engineering Task Force (IETF) were set up to help different projects to collaborate and interface effectively. Thanks to that, when you send an email, there is a protocol (the Internet Message Access Protocol (IMAP)) that allows it to cross different platforms and reach the recipient. At the moment blockchain networks lack similar working interfacing protocols.

4.3   A deeper dive into Bitcoin

Bitcoin is the first blockchain network. It helps facilitate the movement and storage of value on the internet in the form of bitcoins. Each bitcoin is a self-authenticating packet of data and every digital unit is recorded on a shared ledger called the Bitcoin blockchain. It is essential to point out that Bitcoin with capital B is used to refer to the blockchain network while bitcoin with small b refers to the currency.

Bitcoin is a cryptocurrency because its value is secured through cryptography. There is a cap to the number of bitcoins that will be generated of 21 million units. New units of bitcoins come into circulation as a reward to nodes that are securing the network and processing transactions. These nodes are called miners.

The rate at which new bitcoin units come into existence is defined in the protocol. About every ten minutes, new bitcoins are released to one of the miners on the network, this is called a block reward. The number of bitcoins given as a reward halves every few years. At the time of writing this book, the amount released every 10 minutes is 12.5 bitcoins. When the 21 million is reached, sometime in the year 2140, there will be no more new bitcoins.

The Bitcoin network takes a small fee from each transaction. Initially, it was voluntary for the sender to attach a fee. Those who attached a fee had their transactions confirmed faster, but in the end, even those transactions with no fee attached were approved by the network and added on the distributed ledger. However, as the mining reward shrinks, the transaction fee is becoming necessary in order for transactions to be processed.

Miners gain bitcoins as a reward for maintaining the shared ledger, they then sell them to others. To receive, store or send bitcoins you need to have a wallet. A wallet is an application you install on your desktop or mobile phone, but the issue here is that web-based wallets tend to be less secure. A more secure option are hardware wallets. These are devices specifically designed for securing cryptocurrency.

The top challenges that face Bitcoin's global adoption

One of the top challenges for public blockchains is the price volatility of their cryptocurrency. This volatility affects the number of people willing to operate independent nodes and process the transactions that secure the network. If the node operators can't make a profit from their work, they will move on to other activities. Blockchains that can attract and retain enough full nodes are vulnerable to attacks and corruption.

False negative press has also been a major hurdle to adoption. Despite the U.S. Anti-Money Laundering team stating, "the US dollar is still the best way to launder money", crypto is largely associated with illegal activities like Silk Road (a dark online marketplace) and financing illegal activities. The irony is cryptocurrency provides the best line of sight for all transactions in any currency and while some features may appear anonymous, the network is largely available to be culled for identities.

In other words, the premise of anonymity is false. From its early days, Bitcoin and other blockchains have been covered negatively in the mainstream media. The mainstream media has portrayed it as a tool for criminals and other bad actors who want to hide their financial activities from law enforcement. As a result, misinformed regulators have tried to make it difficult to obtain cryptocurrency and have jailed some users.

Another type of negative media has continuously hailed the failure and death of cryptocurrencies. This type of media has incited panic within the cryptocurrency markets and triggered massive sell-offs. While it is hard to measure the extent, many who might find Bitcoin exciting and even useful are made to disregard it even before they begin to explore its potential. A web page known as Bitcoin Obituaries (see: https://99bitcoins.com/bitcoin-obituaries) has been tracking the number of times mainstream media has declared Bitcoin dead or about to die. According to the page, the press has announced Bitcoin's death close to 400 times between 2010 and 2019.

As a greater understanding of how blockchain technology works has developed, the mainstream media has begun to provide a little more favorable coverage. But Bitcoin is still a taboo topic and is often associated with criminal activity. Some acknowledge the usefulness of blockchain technology but have negative feelings about cryptocurrency.

However, the media is not entirely to blame for all the negative coverage cryptocurrency gets. The high number of scams that use Bitcoin in one way or another to steal from the public give the cryptocurrency a bad name, whilst hackers within the space also add to the negative reputation. In early May 2019, Hong Kong-based exchange Bitfinex was exposed as trying to cover a loss of US$850 million by raiding the accounts of their stable coin Tether, a token that is pegged on the dollar. More generally, bad actors stole US$1.7 billion worth of cryptocurrencies from investors in 2018 alone.

Another key issue that public blockchains and especially Bitcoin face is scalability. When the Bitcoin network was launched in January 2009, it could process and confirm about seven transactions per second. In the early days that was enough, and there was no issue. However, as more people started using Bitcoin, the 1MB block capacity strained under the number of new users and soon mempools, a node's holding area for all the pending transactions, were backed up for days. The nearly instant transaction time grounded to a halt and the average transaction cost for using Bitcoin spiked to over US$50 per bitcoin transaction in 2017.

The situation has improved with the adoption of scaling solutions such as SegWit and Lightning Network. However, looking ahead, the problem is not fully solved. The credit card company Visa can process more than 65,000 transactions per second. If the Bitcoin network is to compete as a means of transacting globally, it has to handle nearly as many.

Scaling Bitcoin has turned into a very contentious topic within the open source community who maintain and improve the core software. Things came to a head in 2017 when the community was split into two opposing sides. In fact it was so contentious that it was described as a civil war. One side pushed the increase of the block size from 1MB, and the other fought to keep the size the same. They wanted to decrease the amount of data from each transaction, this was called segregated witness (SegWit). The segregated witness is an off-chain scaling solution that utilizes a secondary layer that processes transaction on the Lightning Network.

Since Bitcoin is not a company with a decision making or governance structure, it was tough to find agreement on how to scale with any of the solutions on the table. On August 1, 2017, the Bitcoin network split into Bitcoin and Bitcoin Cash. Those who didn't want an increase of the block size stayed with Bitcoin (BTC), and those who preferred bigger blocks stood behind Bitcoin Cash (BCH). Even though the Bitcoin network can handle the number of transactions it receives at the moment, it still requires improvement if it is going to compete with traditional payment networks. If it does not scale, then it might never reach critical mass adoption.

Major Bitcoin contributors

Bitcoin is a project run by the community of its users. The first core developer for the Bitcoin blockchain was Satoshi Nakamoto and for a few months after the launch of the project he was the only one. Subsequently, Gavin Andresen and others joined him. When Satoshi left the project in 2010, he appointed Gavin Andresen to take over as the core maintainer.

By May 2019 there were over 350 Bitcoin core contributors listed on Bitcoin.org. The majority of them have contributed a few commits (pieces of code) to the project. However, it happens that the top three Bitcoin core developers, according to the number of commits they have contributed, work on the Bitcoin project full-time thanks to funding from three major entities.

However, anyone with coding skills and great ideas can contribute to the project and help make Bitcoin better. To do that, one has to write a Bitcoin Improvement Proposal (BIP) and publish it for the community to interrogate it. Then they should lead the process of writing the necessary code to implement the change. If the majority of the community thinks it is a useful change, then it is added to the next release of the Bitcoin core software. The following are three top Bitcoin core developers according to commits made on Github:

Wladimir J. van der Laan has the highest number of commits to the Bitcoin project on Github at over 6,000. He took over from Gavin Andresen in April 2014 as the lead developer. His position is to merge patches and other changes to the core software that the community has agreed upon. He is funded by the Digital Currency Initiative (DCI), a project under MIT MediaLlab. MIT Media Lab is a research laboratory at Massachusetts Institute of Technology and in 2016 the DCI announced a US$900,000 Bitcoin Developer Fund for this purpose.

Marco Falke has played a vital role as the primary quality assurance and software tester for Bitcoin core development. He has the second highest number of commits to the project on Github at over 1,700 (2019). Marco started working as a Bitcoin volunteer and has since moved on to work at Chaincode Labs, in New York where he continues to work on Bitcoin projects.

Until 2019, Pieter Wuille has contributed over 1,600 commits to the Bitcoin project on Github. He started to work as a volunteer core developer in 2011, a year after finding out about Bitcoin. He has gone on to become one of the most resourceful contributors. Some of his contributions include Segregated Witness (SegWit), a scaling solution that trims data from each transaction that goes into the Bitcoin block, therefore, creating room for more transactions. Pieter is also credited with implementing hierarchical deterministic wallets, which can automatically generate new public key addresses. This made it easier for Bitcoin users to avoid overusing their public keys and compromising their privacy.

4.4 Hyperledger

Hyperledger is a project that supports several blockchain initiatives, including Hyperledger Fabric. Spun out of the Linux Foundation, Hyperledger was created to help bring standards to blockchain technology that would be tailored for the unique needs of businesses and governments. The core focus is on fostering the development of enterprise-grade and open source "distributed ledger" frameworks and code bases.

Distributed ledger technology (DLT) is categorized within blockchain technology but has three fundamentally distinct differences that are worth noting. These are:

1. No cryptocurrency – the lack of cryptocurrency means that transactions must be processed by nodes that are incentivized to do so because they have an interest in the maintenance of their network and the transactions they are processing.
2. Nodes are known – distributed ledgers are run by nodes that know one another and choose to collaborate. The networks are private and to operate a node you must be granted explicit permission.
3. Development is directed – lead by the Hyperledger Foundation, development is guided in contrast to Bitcoin where development is voluntary and less organized in contribution.

Hyperledger's networks are private but open sourced so you could spin up to your own DLT. It falls into the category of private blockchains, known as permissioned blockchains. To join a private or permissioned blockchain network, an entity has to get permission from an administrator. This is in contrast to a public blockchain network where you do not need permission from anyone to join, since public blockchain networks do not have administrators. Hyperledger directly manages its development and maintenance.

Hyperledger was launched in December 2015 by the Linux Foundation as a consortium project. The foundation partnered with several top technology companies and financial institutions to start the project. The founding members included heavy weights such as IBM, Intel, Cisco, Fujitsu, Hitachi, JP Morgan and Wells Fargo. More members have since joined the consortium and currently, there are close to 300 members.

Fabric is the first blockchain implementation on Hyperledger. It has become the framework for developing many business solutions and is unique within the blockchain ecosystem because it allows developers to use pieces of Fabric without committing to the full blockchain functionality. Fabric is a permissioned blockchain and does not utilize a cryptocurrency. It can be run privately as a tailored plug-and-play blockchain that is fully centralized. It cuts out most of the security features that blockchains use to prevent collusion, which is not always a bad thing depending on your goals for development.

All the participants on Fabric are known, in contrast to a typical public blockchain where all the participants are anonymous by default. It works like most blockchains in that it keeps a ledger of digital "events". These events are structured as transactions and shared among the different participants. The transactions are executed without a cryptocurrency, which again contrasts with a public blockchain that uses its native cryptocurrency to pay the network to operate. Mining nodes are incentivized to secure the network and are rewarded for doing so with cryptocurrency. On Fabric, each node is run by an individual who has an incentive to protect the records and history because it is their own, not because they will receive block rewards.

Even without typical blockchain infrastructure, all transactions are secured, private, and confidential on Fabric. It preserves its integrity by only allowing updates through the consensus of all the participant nodes. This means that when records have been put in, they can never be altered.

Fabric was designed for businesses that need and want a scalable solution and don't want to worry about complying with regulations. All participants must register their identity to membership services to gain access to the system. However, you can have anonymity on Fabric, as it can issue your transactions with derived certificates that are unlinkable to the owning participant and the content of each transaction is encrypted to ensure only the intended participants can make sense of the data.

The Hyperledger Composer is an easy-to-use tool that allows you to create Fabric applications. They are not scalable but can be easily used as proof of concepts (POCs). The best part is that it will enable you to build your blockchain network with JavaScript, one of the most popular development languages in the world. This feature alone will significantly cut down on your need for specialized blockchain developers.

The Composer will decrease the development time and cost and allow you to be production-ready sooner. Another benefit of the Composer is that it utilizes LoopBacks. LoopBacks communicate digital data streams back to your existing business system, thereby keeping your operations in sync. You will still need a good development team to do this, but you can easily mockup your business logic and have your system built.

4.5   EOS's delegated Proof of Stake

EOS is a blockchain platform built to accommodate smart contracts and decentralized applications. Founded after Ethereum, EOS promised to fix many of the limiting factors that had plagued the first two waves of blockchain technology, namely the high cost of Proof of Work and the slow speed associated with having thousands of independent full nodes processing transactions.

While many predecessors to EOS focused on the economics of creating decentralized systems and preserving a permanent record that everyone could access, EOS was more user-centric. The team behind the development of EOS, Block.one, has the belief that blockchain technology must be able to support tens of millions of active daily users. They believe that using a blockchain to secure your application should not be expensive. A third factor they wanted to avoid was the pitfalls of decentralized development. Many blockchains suffer from highly political conflict every time their software upgrades or each time there is a bug that needs to be fixed. Bitcoin and Ethereum have both stalled their development frequently due to infighting.

The EOS team set out to create a new blockchain that:
- Can support millions of active users;
- Is free to use;
- Has fast upgrades and bug recovery;
- Has low latency.

These core beliefs have shaped the structure of EOS significantly. The primary distinguishing feature of EOS is its consensus architecture. It uses Delegated Proof of Stake (DPoS). DPoS is a variation of the Proof of Stake and has been hotly debated. Some developers feel DPoS has a reasonable trade-off in security for scalability and cost reduction while others think that blockchain technology should be as secure and immutable as possible to protect the very nature of the system, based on a permanent record that can be referenced by all.

In EOS's DPoS consensus architecture, the cryptocurrency holders vote for delegates who are responsible for validating transactions and can earn transaction fees for their work. The elected third-party block producers create new blocks and verify transactions for the whole network. EOS concentrates the number of nodes performing this action to 21. By doing so, they increase the speed of the network. The security and integrity of the EOS blockchain are in question, not only because of the limited number of blocks producing nodes but because not all the nodes are required to hold a full history of the EOS blockchain, and it may be possible for a few bad actors to collude and support mutual voting.

Under Delegated Proof of Stake, dishonest block producers are removed by token holders. EOS cryptocurrency holders vote to do this, and their authority is proportional to the percentage of total tokens they hold. Block producing nodes are not required to stake tokens themselves, and this is a differentiating factor from other Proof of Stake consensus architectures that require block producing nodes to stake their own cryptocurrency as a disincentive to fraudulent behavior. In most PoS systems block producers can lose their staked assets if they process transactions that do not conform to the rules of that blockchain. The cryptocurrency holders are not directly compensated for voting but are incentivized to reject bad actors out of preservation of the value and integrity of their cryptocurrency.

The EOS cryptocurrency is used to facilitate smart contracts and DApps. EOS has a considerably different token economic system from other smart contract protocols. The EOS cryptocurrency holders have a right to the network's computational and storage capacity in proportion to their total cryptocurrency holdings. Users do not pay a fee to execute their smart contracts. They only need to hold enough EOS cryptocurrency proportionate to the processing and storage required to complete their smart contract.

EOS started as a white paper in 2017 that was released by a Cayman Island-based crypto company called Block.one. The team raised approximately 7 million Ether. Their raise was valued at a record-breaking US$4 billion. The Block.one team held one of the longest running initial coin offerings (ICOs), ironically on Ethereum, as the means of raising capital.

Founding members of the EOS team include Brendan Blumer and Daniel Larimer. Brendan and Daniel have both been very active in the blockchain space for several years. Brendan founded okay.com, Hong Kong's largest digital property agency. Daniel co-founded several blockchain companies, including decentralized exchange BitShares and the social media network Steemit.

EOS has come a long way since its ICO and is now among the top ten blockchain protocols in the world with one of the largest market capitalizations. It has done some rebranding and is now known as EOSIO. This name change corresponded to a new software update that the Block.one team released.

One of the main reasons that EOS gained so much investor interest is that it addresses some of the many issues concerning the development of a robust DApp ecosystem. While Ethereum is an alternative (and many would consider a competitor), EOS enables the development and hosting of decentralized apps differently, allowing for more scalability, speed, and flexibility. EOS coins do not need to be spent in order to build and run DApps - they simply need to be held.

EOS.io is a blockchain protocol that is a smart contract operating system, and it is known for its user design, as it emulates the actual attributes of a computer as well. One of the many ways that investors believe EOS will change the way that corporations interact is by providing decentralized enterprise solutions that can increase productivity significantly. Owners of EOS tokens can vote on various issues and participate in "on-chain governance" through the blockchain. This allows for more flexibility when it comes to making critical decisions such as freezing, bug fixing of specific apps, and more. EOS also markets itself as being extremely user-friendly for decentralized app developers.

4.6 Ripple

Ripple is one of the most impressive networks for moving and trading value globally. Founded on the concept that money should move as freely and easily as information, Ripple has a low cost, is high security, and is a swift way to trade and exchange value globally. Its infrastructure is being implemented as the framework for new modern banking and trading.

Believe it or not, Ripple is older than Bitcoin. The project has gone through several iterations, but the original implementation was designed by the Canadian developer Ryan Fugger in 2004. Ryan's first iteration was a decentralized monetary system that allowed individuals and communities to set up their own money.

Ripple has grown into a global financial settlement solution that enables banks and consumers to exchange value. Similar to Bitcoin, the Ripple protocol lowers the total cost of settlement by allowing users to transact directly and instantly. It is built on a distributed open source internet protocol, utilizes a consensus ledger, and has a native currency called ripple (XRP). Unlike a public blockchain, not everyone can participate and the nodes that validate transactions on Ripple are tightly controlled. XRP was created all at the same time and is not created through mining blocks.

Ripple's distributed financial technology enables users to send real-time international payments across its networks. Using Ripple, global markets can meet the demand for fast, low-cost, and on-demand comprehensive payment services.

Ripple is particularly good at cross-border payments and exchanging two dissimilar things of value. It has created a global network of financial institutions, market makers and consumers who now trade any type of value anywhere in the world, instantly.

Ripple has had to fight several battles with regulators because of the disruption it has created in the banking industry. FinCEN fined Ripple US$700,000 for secrecy act violations. The fine was for selling XRP to Roger Ver, a well-known Bitcoin investor, and failing to file a suspicious activity report because Roger had a felony conviction for selling fireworks on eBay.

The best way to describe Ripple is as an exchange network and a trading platform with a blockchain backend. Where most blockchains operate without knowing the identity of other users, Ripple controls who can access their blockchain. There are two main ways to interact on the Ripple network. The financial users of the system participate in the network by issuing, accepting, and trading assets to facilitate payments. The other way is as a node operator. Ripple only allows a handful of nodes, and the identities of the operators are all known. The nodes keep track of transactions and come to a consensus about the validity and order of those transactions with the other nodes in the network.

Unlike Bitcoin, that does not require users to trust or know other individuals on the network, the whole infrastructure of Ripple requires that all parties trust and know one another to some extent. A financial participant must trust the issuers of assets it holds, and a node operator must trust that the other nodes in its validator list will not to collude to block valid transactions from being confirmed. It is all about trust and aligned incentives for cooperation.

XRP is the cryptocurrency of the Ripple network; it has an added function that other cryptocurrencies don't possess. It is used to facilitate trade between two dissimilar things of value that have a low trading volume and no trusted path on the Ripple network. Between the nodes, the network, and the financial participant, Ripple has built the basic infrastructure that optimizes the modern payment process and exchange globally.

Ripple has been replacing some central bank functionality through software. It acts as a neutral transaction protocol that allows banks and payment networks to have a shared ledger. This enables them to clear transactions in five seconds. It gives users continuous connectivity between each other, and it has constant monitoring of the flow of transactions across the network.

Banks are very excited about this technology because it allows them to move away from intermediaries and clearing houses to a faster, cheaper, and less risky system. Banks have dramatically sped up the process of cross-border payments by removing the need for paper and intermediaries.

The main characteristics of Ripple are:
- Does real-time payments;
- Does comprehensive transaction traceability;
- Does near-instant reconciliation;
- Has the ability to convert almost any type of currency, commodity, or token.

It is important to realize that Ripple is significantly different from Bitcoin in its structure and the way the network operates. Ripple finds the most efficient exchange route, structuring transactions as debts, and uses its cryptocurrency as the exchange mechanism between the different types of value that it are traded on the Ripple network.

A major difference is that Ripple is all about trust, whereas for the most part other blockchains are about trustless systems. In Bitcoin, any two parties can send one another bitcoin tokens, and the network then validates that no one is cheating in that transaction. Part of the way Bitcoin balances every block of transactions is to check to make sure that all the tokens involved have only been spent once.

Another significant difference, that comes from trust, is that Ripple does not use Proof of Work consensus. The Ripple team has eliminated the large power burden needed by most blockchains to secure themselves, and in doing so, they use significantly less electricity. Removing these traditional features also makes Ripple faster.

Not your average blockchain
It is easy to see that Ripple works very differently from other blockchains. One of the most noteworthy differences is how the network is decentralized and comes to consensus.

The nature of decentralization in Ripple is subtle. A node can put any other node it wants into its validator list to listen to what transactions those nodes want to confirm. The only requirement is that there is sufficient overlap between each node in the validator list, so the network doesn't accidentally come to multiple different consensuses.

The way Ripple manages that now is to have each node maintain its validator list, including Ripple's nodes. This ensures there is sufficient overlapping. As the node's network grows, its list will include more and more validators from well-known trustworthy and independent institutions around the world. Over time Ripple's consensus process will become more and more decentralized.

It is important to keep in mind that Ripple is made for moving money faster and cheaper. This is a very heavily regulated area of the economy. Ripple states clearly that it is the only software that enables you to perform these tasks. It is completely up to you to understand and comply with regulations.

Ripple, like other blockchains which work through cryptocurrencies, has many dangers. I've listed a few below that are unique to Ripple. However, it is best to always use common sense while working in the cryptocurrency world and follow all other security best practices described in this book. It truly is the new Wild West, full of opportunity and risk.

Possible dangers of using Ripple
As described earlier, Ripple was created to move value across the world cheaper and faster than any other network. The structure of Ripple works with clusters of markets. These markets have trusted nodes confirming transactions together. There are small price differences between these groups at times, and these price differences attract unethical trading.

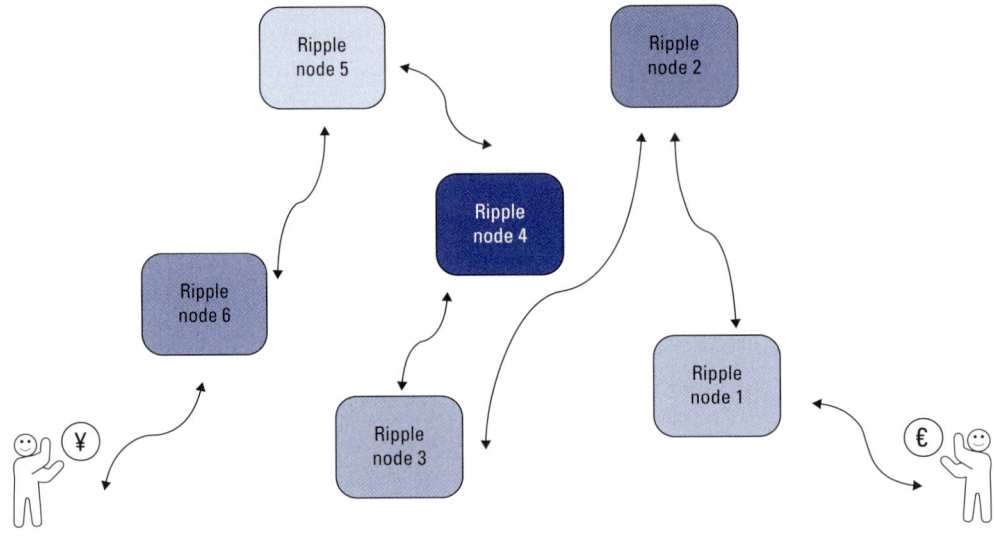

Figure 23 Ripple – exchanging two things of value across the Ripple network.

The Ripple network, in particular, is prone to arbitrage because it has many currencies and multiple markets, and smart programmers can manipulate the order of transactions. The two better known forms of this on Ripple are advantageous arbitrage transaction placement and large trade front running.

Advantageous arbitrage transaction placement is taking advantage of a price difference between multiple markets before the ledger closes. This happens every five seconds, so traders utilize arbitrage bots to exploit the market. These bots strike a combination of matching deals that capitalize on the small imbalances between the markets and push their transactions into an optimal position within the ledger. The traders then profit by taking the difference in the price of these markets.

In addition, the structure and latency in Ripple's consensus expose the network to a new type of front running of large trades. It is possible to do this because each node in the network broadcasts transactions to other trusted nodes. During this time, bots will be monitoring all transactions for opportunities to jump in front of large trades.

The bot will buy up initial offers to fulfill the large purchase and then upsell them to the original owner. At the same time, it repositions the transactions within the ledger to allow this to happen. The net result of this behavior is that the original owner will receive less value in the trade.

Ripple is committed to removing exploits from its network and has an open offer for programmers to earn money through hunting down bugs, exploits, and vulnerabilities. It is highly likely that these two bugs will be fixed shortly.

4.7 Unearthing Ethereum

Ethereum is one of the most advanced and accessible blockchains in the world. It offers developers tools to build just about anything they can imagine. One of the most potent uses of Ethereum has been its smart contracts and specifically the smart contracts that conform to the ERC20 ruleset. ERC20 smart contracts on Ethereum have allowed thousands of new blockchain projects to be funded through initial coin offerings (ICO).

Ethereum is an industry leader in blockchain innovation. It is pushing the boundaries in what is possible on a shared, global, and accessible network. Ethereum is a completely public and fully distributed blockchain that allows anyone in the world, who has of course not been limited by their government, to participate at any level in the development and use. Understanding this technology is essential because it's leading the charge in smart contracts, decentralized organizations, and token offerings.

Exploring the brief history of Ethereum

Ethereum started as a whitepaper in 2013 primarily written by Vitalik Buterin, from Russia and only a 19 year-old at the time. Vitalik was working in the Bitcoin community as a writer and programmer and wanted to expand the functionality of blockchain technology. Vitalik recognized that there were significantly more applications for blockchain than the ability to move value without a central authority.

The Bitcoin blockchain community at that time was fiercely debating the network being "bloated" by lots of low-value transactions from the first wave of decentralized applications. These applications were producing a tremendous amount of small transactions due to securing themselves on Bitcoin's blockchain and piggybacking on the miners' need to keep a complete history. Miners disliked this practice as it taxed their storage, and some Bitcoin users disliked it as it increased the cost and time for confirmation of their bitcoin transaction.

Vitalik and many other developers, however, believed that decentralized applications would be revolutionary. The massive code overhaul needed to make this possible on Bitcoin was too politically charged to change. Vitalik's project in Bitcoin was the "colored coin" project, wherein he with Or Perelman and others were trying to institute scripting within Bitcoin. However, the transaction size limited the project's capabilities.

Vitalik together with a handful of other developers decided that they needed to build a new blockchain that would be designed primarily for applications. Vitalik and his team of developers and business people established the Ethereum Foundation in early 2014. They raised US$18 million in funding through one of the first ICOs. Many have passionately debated if ICOs are illegal because they are an unlicensed security offering, since investors believe that their investment in the tokens will increase in value. The Securities and Exchange Commission (SEC) in the United States has given Ethereum approval on their ICO but has repeatedly and strongly warned all other entrepreneurs who hope to raise capital from the public that they must register.

After raising funds for Ethereum, the foundation hired a large development team to build it. They dispensed with most of the business team who went on to form another company called ConsenSys that produces applications on Ethereum.

The first release of the Ethereum blockchain network was called Frontier and went live in July 2015. It was a bare-bones software release and was difficult to use to build applications. Homestead, a more user-friendly version of Ethereum, was made available in 2016. It allowed anyone with a little programming skill to utilize the application template. It was the release of Homestead that allowed a broader community to build and grow applications and increased the popularity of blockchain technology. A year after its release, the blockchain space saw an explosion of new foundations and companies all built on Ethereum and specifically the ERC20 smart contracts that allowed them to raise capital through an ICO.

Ethereum has gone through another transformation as it has continued to expand and decentralize its operations and development. The foundation's mindset is counter-intuitive to how most organizations function. They believe that to successfully foster a vibrant decentralized ecosystem, they must deliberately apply a philosophy of subtraction. The idea of subtraction is to resist the natural tendency to grow and accumulate value within one's self or organization. Instead, an organization fosters the creation of value outside the organization and across the ecosystem.

Ethereum Serenity is the current (2019) name of the development that Ethereum is undergoing. It will include a series of planned upgrades that will allow Ethereum to reduce complexity and continue to operate even if a large portion of nodes go offline. It will also allow Ethereum to upgrade to quantum secure code as it becomes available. It is working on increasing decentralization by allowing a typical consumer laptop to process and validate transactions. These upgrades will be rolled out incrementally over several years but have begun already.

The first of these is the ETH 1.x initiative that is focused on improving Ethereum's short term scalability and sustainability to ease the transition to ETH 2.0. An essential part of this upgrade may be the ZK-rollup. It is a zero-knowledge proof to enable Ethereum to achieve hundreds of transactions per second. A zero-knowledge proof is a cryptography method by which one party can prove to another party that they know something without conveying anything except that they know the value.

Another effort from Ethereum on their philosophy of "subtraction" has been the support of Ethereum Academic and Research Collaboration and ETHGlobal. They host hackathons and research around the world. They have special efforts with Stanford and MIT that support research in mathematicians, computer scientists and economists.

The open and collaborative efforts of thousands of people have made Ethereum one of the most complex blockchains ever created. It has several of its own Turing-complete programming languages. Turing-complete means a programing language can be used to create any type of software you can imagine.

The power of the new Turing-complete programming languages allows developers to create any application they want and are only limited by the economics and speed of the Ethereum network. The implementation of Eth 2.0 will negate the cost and speed restrictions of the current state of Ethereum. The new programming languages closely resemble popular programming languages such as JavaScript and Python.

The Ethereum ecosystem is currently the best place to build decentralized applications. All other blockchains have limited the number of nodes to cut cost and increase speed. The Ethereum community has worked very hard to have impressive documentation and more user-friendly interfaces than many other Blockchains. It is still very important to remember that Ethereum is under constant development and that it can be an unstable environment. Many may prefer a private version of Ethereum as a way to control decentralized development.

Even though Ethereum is one of the most well-known cryptocurrencies, and many believe that it even has the potential to overtake Bitcoin at some point, the truth is that there are still many challenges when it comes to partnerships and overall mass adoption concerning Ethereum.

First and foremost, while Ethereum might be able to offer a more transparent alternative to current solutions in many sectors, some have a very simple criticism: Ethereum might be too slow. When one considers that Ethereum can only handle somewhere around 20 transactions per second - it is hard to imagine that it can revolutionize the financial sector when credit card giants such as Visa can process thousands of transactions per second. There are some who wonder how Ethereum can be revolutionary if it might not be able to handle transactions as efficiently as the current legacy systems.

Since Ethereum is one of the most well-known cryptocurrencies, it faces the issue of regulation from the SEC. And although a top SEC official, William Hinman, recently stated that Ethereum is most likely not going to be prosecuted for securities violations, a concrete decision has not been made yet. The SEC Chairman Jay Clayton appeared to agree with

Hinman's statement, but this does not mean that Ethereum will necessarily be free from traditional securities oversight.

The other main issue is how Ethereum will scale when it comes to mass adoption. While Ethereum cannot exist as a "world computer" currently, there are many who believe that the vibrant community of developers has already anticipated this issue, and there are various scalability solutions in the offing. There are solutions that are both focused on how to scale Ethereum itself and how to move transactions to a second layer in order to increase overall efficiency.

4.8 The Waves platform – a Russian blockchain

The Waves platform is one of the easiest blockchains to use. It has an intuitive wallet that has a built-in decentralized peer-to-peer exchange, a voting system, a messaging and chat function, and a decentralized domain name system. Many blockchains have one or two of these features, but Waves has all of them. It lets you start using and creating your cutting-edge decentralized applications (DApps) with an easy download and a few clicks. Many believe that Waves will be integral when it comes to building a blockchain infrastructure that will benefit both the public and private sector.

Founded in 2016 by Russian physicist Sacha Ivanov, the project has grown substantially. Waves raised approximately 30,000 BTC, about US$18 million at that time, to create the platform. Sacha has since gathered one of the largest communities and claims to have 300,000 active users in 25 countries. Waves has a dedicated team of 100 developers in Russia who are continually improving the platform.

Based on the Nxt Proof-of-Stake protocol, the Waves platform is a fully public blockchain that is decentralized, transparent, and auditable. It is different from other blockchains that use smart contract infrastructure, like Ethereum, or are forks of the Bitcoin Blockchain. One of the key differences is that Waves allows you to create colored coins. When you create a colored coin, you are associating the information with an address, as opposed to creating smart contracts that you have programmed for that specific purpose. Colored coins can be used to represent anything you might want to trade on a blockchain. Things like stocks, bonds, commodities, and real estate can all be expressed. You can create your own in a few minutes on Waves.

It is always important to remember that just because you can create tokens and colored coins, this does not mean that it is legal to distribute them, especially if they are a financial instrument or represent an investment. Always check with your legal counsel before creating something that may be used as a financial instrument.

Waves secures its network by leveraging the balances of existing accounts to "forge" blocks. Instead of nodes "mining" new blocks to earn cryptocurrency, the platform rewards cryptocurrency holders for validating blocks. The validating nodes are called "forgers" and are given transaction fees rather than a block reward. The Proof-of-Stake (PoS) algorithm has become popular because it is cheaper to operate and can even be run on small devices like the Raspberry Pi.

It is essential to understand the differences between consensus systems for blockchains. As you may remember, these are the set of rules that govern how a blockchain operates. Specifically, many PoW blockchains are vulnerable to a 51% attack where a majority of the mining power is being generated by a few individuals who can then corrupt the records written in the history of the blockchain's ledger. PoS systems, like Waves, have their issues. It's possible for a few individuals to amass a majority of the Waves cryptocurrency and take over the network. When you are evaluating a blockchain, it is always essential to consider the cost, speed, and security you need for your business.

Waves is well positioned to be a significant platform for fast and easy asset tokenization. The ICO craze of 2017 left a bad taste in many people's mouths regarding tokenization because there was a lot of fraud. Waves is helping change the public's perception of the cryptocurrency markets by fostering trust in the crypto space and increasing token transparency through its BetterTokens project. They are developing due diligence standards for companies that are tokenizing assets.

The Waves team is improving investor protection and regulatory compliance. Part of their work involves having an expert committee that assesses token issuers' projects. Those who have qualified are recognized on Waves Decentralized Exchange (DEX) with a ticker.

Waves Decentralized Exchange (DEX)
Waves Decentralized Exchange (DEX) allows you to trade assets from the security of your wallet. Because the Waves wallet supports several different types of cryptocurrency, you can trade them all on the Waves DEX, not just the Waves cryptocurrency and Waves colored coins.

The Waves DEX has fixed one of the many issues that have kept DEXs from being more widely used. They have created real-time trading by centralizing the order book matcher. This allows them to connect buyers and sellers more easily. The Waves DEX is a hybrid of both centralized and decentralized exchange technology. It's centralized matching engine pairs incoming orders and executes your trades typically within milliseconds. This is an advantage over other DEXs that are fully integrated within a blockchain. Fully decentralized exchanges are dependent on the block time speed of their blockchain and have much higher trading costs. You may still have liquidity issues as DEXs do not have a full marketplace ecosystem such as market makers and takers who help keep prices stable.

On the Waves DEX, you signal your willingness to purchase or sell assets by creating, signing, and sending a limited order request to the Waves matcher. An order for a buy is a set number of a token at a price equal to or greater than you have stipulated. When you create a new order, it is sent to the DEX. Your order is then checked for accuracy, and the validity of your signature. It is validated by your wallet's public key.

The orders on the Waves DEX are linked in pairs and checked by Waves nodes. Then the matcher creates an exchange transaction; it will sign the transaction and record the trade in the Waves blockchain. You don't have to execute a full order because the matcher can pair partial orders. The validating nodes do not charge these unfinished orders a full order fee. Your assets are only transferred after the trade has been published in the Waves blockchain. If the matcher fails for some reason, your trade will be canceled, and all unfilled orders are canceled automatically after 30 days.

Waves has made some high-profile partnerships, including with the accounting firm Deloitte, one of the largest professional financial services firms in the world. The point of the partnership is to offer institutional clients a chance to provide initial coin offering (ICO) options and customized blockchain solutions.

The Waves blockchain does have many challenges to overcome if it is to meet its ambition. There is a concern that it is too Russia-centric to reach its full potential on a global scale. It is no secret that the Russian economy can be insular; politics have been heated. Because Waves is entirely embedded with Russia, and many of its strategic partnerships involve Russian companies rather than global companies, it may not gain traction in other countries.

4.9 Summary

There are hundreds of blockchains and thousands of blockchain projects, and this is growing by the day. This chapter has only covered a fraction of the most exciting, promising, and popular initiatives that are currently up and running.

Other initiatives that will warrant your attention in the future include Facebook's new Libra initiative. This will be a private blockchain that is building on the work other efforts have already tested. It will utilize a token, offer complete programming languages that allow for DApp creation and, perhaps most significantly, there is the possibility that all Facebook's existing customers will be onboarded into the Libra ecosystem.

The future economic business models and industries are being born now, thanks to the convergence of several older technologies that are used to create blockchains. The most apparent use cases are identity, tokenization, cross-border payment, and decentralized applications. Each of these innovations has sparked new industries in their own right. And it is highly likely that even more innovations and groundbreaking changes will occur in the next generation of blockchain technology.

4.10 Test your knowledge

1. **What are four of the primary use cases for blockchain technology?**
   A. Four primary use cases of blockchain technology: storage, digital identity, transfer of value, and decentralized applications.
   B. Four primary use cases of blockchain technology: tokenization, digital identity, store of value, and centralized applications.
   C. Four primary use cases of blockchain technology: tokenization, digital identity, transfer of value, and decentralized applications.
   D. Four primary use cases of blockchain technology: gaming, fraud, ICOs, and applications.

2. **Is it illegal to trade bitcoin in some countries?**
   A. Yes
   B. No

3. **What was the first blockchain network?**
   A. The first network was Ripple.
   B. The first network was Ethereum.
   C. The first network was Waves.
   D. The first network was Bitcoin.

4. **Did Bitcoin do an initial coin offering?**
   A. Yes
   B. No

5. **Is it free to use Bitcoin and send transactions?**
   A. Yes
   B. No

6. **Hyperledger is a public blockchain.**
   A. Yes
   B. No

7. **What is the name of the cryptocurrency that Hyperledger mines?**
   A. Hyperledger mines Hyper.
   B. Hyperledger mines HXP.
   C. Hyperledger does not use a cryptocurrency.
   D. Hyperledger mines cryptocurrencies from Bitcoin, Ethereum, and Ripple.

8. **What type of consensus architecture does EOS support?**
   A. EOS's consensus architecture is Delegated Proof of Authority.
   B. EOS's consensus architecture is Delegated Proof of Work.
   C. EOS's consensus architecture is Proof of Stake.
   D. EOS's consensus architecture is Delegated Proof of Stake.

9. **How many validating nodes does EOS have?**
   A. EOS has 11 dedicated nodes.
   B. EOS has 21 dedicated nodes.
   C. EOS has 31 dedicated nodes.
   D. EOS has 51 dedicated nodes.

10. **Can you mine XRP on the Ripple network?**
    A. Yes
    B. No

11. **What is ERC20?**
    A. ERC20 is a token standard for the Ethereum network that allows developers to create tokens that are interoperable with multiple wallets and exchanges.
    B. ERC20 is the consensuses algorithm for the Ethereum network.
    C. ERC20 is the native cryptocurrency for the Ethereum network.
    D. ERC20 is a regulatory body that oversees security offerings on the Ethereum network.

12. **Ethereum introduced which major innovation to blockchain technology?**
    A. Ethereum was the first ICO and allowed thousands of people to raise capital using ERC20 tokens.
    B. Ethereum was the very first blockchain.
    C. Ethereum has multiple Turing-complete programming languages. This innovation allows developers to create any application they want inside a blockchain.
    D. Ethereum use a multialgorithm approach to mining bitcoins. This innovation allows developers to secure more blocks faster.

13. **The Waves platform secures itself with which type of consensus algorithm and network structure?**
    A. Waves is 10% Proof-of-Stake (PoS) and 90% Proof-of-Work (PoW) public blockchain. Waves secures the network by leveraging the balances of existing accounts to "forge" blocks.
    B. Waves is 100% Proof-of-Stake (PoS) public blockchain. Waves secures the network by leveraging the balances of existing accounts to "forge" blocks.
    C. Waves secures the network by leveraging the balances of existing accounts to "mine" blocks.
    D. Waves is a private blockchain. Waves secures the network by having dedicated audit nodes.

14. What is a DEX?
   A. A DEX is a Decentralized exchange that allows you to trade assets from a centralized exchange.
   B. A DEX is a chat platform that allows you to trade assets and talk with other token holders.
   C. A DEX is a Distributed exchange that allows you to trade assets from the security of your wallet.
   D. A DEX is a Decentralized exchange that allows you to trade assets from the security of your wallet.

5 Second generation applications of Blockchain technology

In this chapter you will explore the second-generation applications of blockchain technology. These are exciting for their many commercial and social uses. Blockchain applications are primarily known as a "back end" technology and are distributed databases. The applications you will learn about now are the technologies that are built on top of, or in some case inside, blockchains that are consumer-facing.

Understanding these new and emerging technologies is essential because they are leading to changes in government and financial technology, and online security. The next generation of applications of blockchain are as varied as any application of software and may already be affecting your life.

The chapter will cover smart contracts, tokens, decentralized applications, and decentralized autonomous organizations. You will learn about the key differences between cryptocurrency and tokens and uncover the limitations of smart contracts.

5.1 Smart contracts

Smart contracts may be one of the most important innovations in software you will encounter. It is, therefore, important to understand how they work and the limitations they currently have in deployment. A smart contract acts as an online contract between two or more parties. You should note that the word "contract" has no legal meaning in this context. It is not binding in the same sense as a business contract. There are some significant differences between what code inside a smart contract can do now and the laws that enforce traditional contracts.

Smart contracts are created by developers and enforced with Boolean logic, mathematics, and encryption. A legally binding contract, on the other hand, is created by a lawyer and enforced by a judicial system.

Smart contacts have automated performance and verification. For example, you could create an automated energy contract to buy power when the price reaches a predetermined rate. You could do this using a smart contract by programming it to listen to a data feed from a wind turbine or some other connected device. The code in your contract would execute once a pre-specified action or event occurred.

You could have a traditional contract to buy energy at a given price, but you would need to rely on a person to execute the contract, and if you or the other party failed to hold up their part of the contract the judicial system would step in to enforce action.

Enforcement of smart contracts have many limitations at this time. They can only enforce, or rather take action on what is within their domain. For example, you could create a smart contract bond that stated you would release a piece of digital art once a specified amount of cryptocurrency was sent to a pre-specified address. You cannot force another party to release funds.

Legal contracts are enforced by a judicial system; they don't have the same limitations as smart contracts. If you violate a court order to pay somebody, even in a civil lawsuit, you can be charged with contempt and go to prison, or funds can be automatically withdrawn from your account. Laws are more flexible, and software is more rigid. Laws and contracts are interpreted by people who have legal options. Code is usually only interpreted one way, and if it executes unexpectedly it means there is a bug that needs to be fixed.

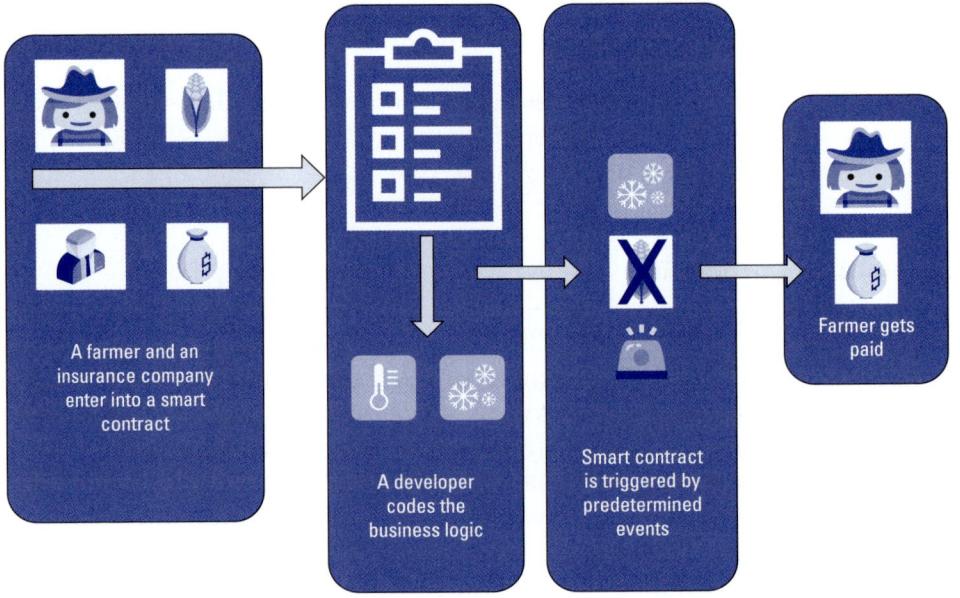

Figure 24 Smart contract – a farming smart contract can ensure insurance payments are made automatically. If the temperature goes down and damages crops the farmer will receive payment.

That said, smart contracts have the potential to automate and reduce costs. In the case of a simple agreement, this can be contained within a blockchain system where your contract can perform and verify a pre-specified event. There are a wide range of use cases and the microtransaction capability of smart contracts that are built-in automatically with public blockchains makes smart contracts very interesting.

Smart contracts: origins and how they function

Nick Szabo, a computer scientist, legal scholar, and cryptographer is credited with having coined the term in the 1990s in his work in digital contracts and digital currency. He has broken down the concept of smart contracts into a set of promises that have been specified in digital form and include protocols which allow the two parties to perform their promises.

With the development of Ethereum blockchain, smart contracts have taken on more meaning and applications. They have become immutable computer programs that run deterministically within a virtual machine (VM) and are part of the blockchain network protocol.

Let's unwrap that last sentence a bit. Immutable in the context of a smart contract means that once you have deployed a smart contract, it cannot be modified. This is unlike traditional software that is centralized and allows an administrator to amend and fix bugs at any time. Of course, there are exceptions, such as smart contracts that have an administrative function. But usually a smart contract can only be modified by deploying a new instance of the contract. There are new protocols that have changed this norm, including EOS and Hyperledger Fabric. Both offer more centralized controls that enable developers to change contracts at will. And whilst there are certain use cases for why modification may be necessary, most of the appeal of a decentralized contract is that it can't be changed after agreement on the conditions for execution.

Because smart contracts are interpreted by computers that are reading Boolean logic, mathematics, and encryption, the execution of the contract should always be the same, in other words it is deterministic. The outcome is the same for every time it is run.

A virtual machine creates a contained environment that enables you to create and run smart contracts, and it is constrained. Smart contracts can only access their state, the transaction that called it, and some information from past transactions that are stored in the blockchain the smart contract is written on.

Creating and deploying smart contracts

Smart contracts are written in high-level computer languages, since these are a little easier to read and write to people. Many blockchains have developed their own unique programming languages that are tailored for smart contract creation. Solidity, an Ethereum blockchain programming language, is very popular, and it resembles the high-level programming language JavaScript.

However, the blockchain will not be able to read your contract, so you will need to take another step. Your smart contract must be translated or rather compiled into bytecode. Bytecode is code designed to be interpreted by the VM. Once compiled, you can deploy it on a blockchain by creating and sending a special type of transaction.

Another interesting thing you can do with smart contracts is to layer them so that one contract can call another contract. By doing this, you can create a chain of execution that allows you to have different outcomes based on different inputs. Many blockchains allow you to call any public contract within their ecosystem. This means you can create contracts that build on other people's work.

It is important for you to know that within smart contracts there are two types of accounts. The first type are accounts that you can control through private keys. These are known as externally owned accounts (EOA). It is with an EOA that all smart contracts are initiated. The second type of account is controlled by the code you wrote within your smart contract. Contracts will lie dormant, and will listen for an event, such as the sending funds from one address to another, that will then trigger execution.

Ethereum was primarily developed for smart contract construction but Bitcoin, along with almost all other blockchains, supports smart contracts, or their own unique version of smart contracts. The smart contracts allow users to, in essence, transfer data, often representing "value" such as a cryptocurrency, a music file, or some other scarce digital resource from one user to another. Meanwhile, the nodes from that blockchain network validate the transactions and ensure both parties cooperate as they had previously agreed within their smart contract.

The Bitcoin blockchain is less known for smart contracts, but the white paper that originally proposed the Bitcoin network alluded to their creation. Smart contracts on Bitcoin use what is known as "opcode", which was introduced by Peter Todd as Bitcoin Improvement Proposal (BIP) 65. Opcode on Bitcoin makes it possible, for example, to write smart contracts that prevent funds in a multi-signature wallet from being spent until specific criteria have been met.

Particl.io is an influential leader in smart contract development on Bitcoin and is a non-profit Swiss foundation. They are creating an open-source and decentralized privacy platform for the creation of decentralized applications that was designed to work with any cryptocurrency.
Hyperledger and several of its projects such as Hyperledger Fabric, Hyperledger Sawtooth and Hyperledger Iroha are important private and permissioned blockchain tools that make the process easier for the creation of smart contracts.

Hyperledger Fabric is, at this point, the most developed project and has the best tutorials that are geared towards business use cases. Within a few minutes you should be able to test out and learn a few things using Fabric, even if you are a novice.

5.2 Tokens

Tokens are self-authenticating data packets that represent a rare digital bit of information. Tokens gain the ability to represent themselves and prove authenticity automatically because they are generated on a blockchain. The immutable and linear histories stored on blockchains prevent fraud.

Tokens are generated normally in one of two ways. The first tokens were created by sending a special transaction on Bitcoin that had a small message. The message stated that some new assets had been created and were credited to a Bitcoin address. Later, other blockchains developed more complex transactions that created tokens. The Ethereum Foundation pioneered and greatly improved token technology, building a framework for the programming of tokens and allowing them to be used for more complex tasks.

Cryptocurrency is like a token but is generated differently. The primary distinction and a good rule of thumb for knowing if you are dealing with a token or a cryptocurrency is to ask a simple question. Was "it" generated as a mining reward for securing a network? Another useful distinction is that tokens are normally generated all at once when a smart contract or colored coin transaction creates them. Cryptocurrencies, on the other hand, are generated over time autonomously by the blockchain network. This, however, is not a hard and fast rule as smart contracts allow for all kinds of functionality and could generate tokens over time too.

Another thing you should be aware of is that not all blockchain networks have cryptocurrency, but all such networks allow for the issuance of tokens. Tokens, like a cryptocurrency, can act as a bearer instrument. They can be used to transfer value between two parties over a blockchain network and can be used to represent rare digital assets or even real-world assets. It's important to note that tokens are very flexible and may not be bearer instruments.

The difference between a cryptocurrency and a token lies in the reason they are created. A token is created by a single party that would like to account for something of value. This may be a payment coupon, stock in a company, or licenses for software. In contrast, a blockchain network generates a cryptocurrency as a reward mechanism for nodes that facilitate the upkeep of its shared database. Cryptocurrencies are generated over time by the blockchain's algorithm and in response to actions taken on the blockchain network. Tokens are often generated all at once.

Token standards
There are many types of tokens, and Ethereum, EOS, Waves, and Hyperledger Fabric, among many others, have created many tools standards for tokens. The shared standards on Ethereum are to be thanked for a whole new generation of blockchain technology. One of their most popular token standards, the ERC-20, has allowed billions of dollars of capital to be raised globally through token sales.

The ERC-20 token standard is the most common token on the Ethereum network, and other blockchains have adopted the same rule set for their tokens. One of the driving factors in its popularity was the fact that ERC-20 tokens made it easy for anyone with a little coding skill to create a new project and collect funds. These funding events were called initial coin offerings (ICOs).

The ERC-721 is another popular token standard. It differs from the ERC-20 in that each token is unique whereas ERC-20 tokens generated from the same contract are interchangeable. A common use for the ERC-721 is digital collectibles. It allows an issuer to prove uniqueness and transferability of a digital asset while allowing each asset to be unique. Cryptokitties (https://www.cryptokitties.co) was the first ERC-721 implementation.

Second generation tokens

Tokens saw a surge in popularity in 2017 and 2018, though recently interest has faltered due to the high level of fraud and the failure of many projects.

However, a new spin on tokens has begun to gain a footing that addresses some of the core questions about the innate value of a token, such as what does it mean to own something "rare" and is it rare enough when it is just software? The two direction that tokens have taken are referred to as stable coins and security tokens.

A stable coin ties its value to that of another asset such as a government-issued currency. Interoperability between cryptocurrency and traditional financial instruments is a massive issue across blockchains. Stable coins are a way for the old and new worlds of finance to meet. They interface with traditional fiat systems and offer a more palatable instrument that looks and feels similar to fiat currency. The first stable coin that gained a footing was Tether back in 2014, originally called Realcoin. The concept is simple, keep funds in a bank account that are equal to the number of Tether. However, it has had a rocky road with questions on transparency in terms of whether it had held the equivalent currencies in reserve. In addition it had a system breach in 2017, and a hacker made off with over US$30 million worth of Tether.

Another fascinating development is the U.S. government regulation of 1:1 currency tokens. Gemini, Circle and a few others established a crypto exchange 1:1 US dollar token that is regulated by the U.S. government and is audited by a third party. With withering trust in Tether, this is a welcome reprieve for crypto traders who would like the stability of US dollars and the fluidity of a token.

Stable tokens may be able to experience the same explosion in popularity thanks to the work of companies like Silamoney.com that has created an application programming interface (API) platform with a developer suite that issues stable coins on Ethereum blockchain called Sila tokens.

Security tokens (STOs) are tied to the value of an outside asset such as equity in a company, ownership of a bond, or even a commodity like oil. The Venezuela Petro token is an exciting development as it is both issued by a sovereign government and was backed by oil, the country's greatest commodity. The Petro was met with a high level of skepticism, indeed President Trump banned U.S. citizens from buying Venezuelan cryptocurrency. Unfortunately, corruption in Venezuela prevented the Petro from gaining much traction and sadly this was used by the Venezuelan government as an excuse to raid the bank accounts of its citizens.

5.3 Decentralized applications

Decentralized applications - often just referred to as DApps - are applications that run on a P2P (peer-to-peer) network instead of a single system. DApps can be tools, programs, games, and more that connect users and providers directly. You have probably already used one - BitTorrent, Popcorn Time, BitMessage and Tor are all traditional DApps that don't utilize a blockchain.

DApps expand smart contracts beyond simple A-to-B value transfers. DApps are built with smart contracts but use other services such as secure messaging and often allow an unlimited number of participants to interact within a given rule set. Dappradar.com is one of the best places to find new and popular DApps. There you can find an ever-growing list of games, exchanges, and marketplaces.

How are DApps constructed?
DApps work much like traditional web apps. They will utilize common web programming languages such as HTML, CSS, and JavaScript to render their web pages. But instead of calling a conventional centralized database with an API, a DApp will call a blockchain smart contract. DApps have their whole back-end running on a P2P blockchain network.

It is easy to remember that the "front-end" of an application is what you see and the "back-end" is where the magic happens. It is all the mathematics and logic that allow you to interact with an application. Smart contracts are the "back-end" and often only make up a small part of a DApp.

Usually DApps will minimize their need to interact with a blockchain for two practical reasons. Each smart contract execution has a monetary cost and can reduce the application's speed. The transaction fee can add up and the more times your application requires the execution of a smart contract, the more expensive running the application becomes and the longer your user may need to wait. Some new blockchain protocols, such as EOS, are looking to reduce that cost. Every blockchain at this point is in wrapped development and their developers are working hard to solve these scaling problems.

The front-end of DApps can be decentralized but it doesn't have to be. Some will choose to use decentralized storage such as the offerings from Swarm or IPFS (InterPlanetary File System) to secure their entire application more thoroughly.

There is a philosophical distinction between open source and closed source software. Open source allows anyone with the appetite and aptitude to look at every line of code you have written. You usually keep it in your GitHub account and other developers can use your code for non-commercial purposes under an MIT or Apache license. Closed source software is kept private. There are strong monetary reasons to not share your code. It could be the edge in your business over the competition or a source of income from the sale of licenses.

Controversy over open and closed source software comes into play frequently in blockchain because on the one hand, it is essential to verify the blockchain code is sound and the very public nature of the code makes it stronger as engineers constantly build and improve on it. Blockchains are wonderful foundations to build businesses and these businesses tend to like to keep software they have developed proprietary. DApps are interesting as they require developers to make choices regarding how much code they will expose.

DApps are divided into three broad categories based on their function:
- DApps that manage money;
- DApps that utilize money but are built for another purpose, such as a game;
- Apps for governance, such as a voting system. These governance applications are called "decentralized autonomous organizations" which is normally just shortened to DAOs.

Ethereum hosted the first DAO for managing an investment fund. Sadly, it is most known for being hacked and in trying to solve the DAO hack, the Ethereum community was split into two groups - those who wanted to regain the lost funds and those who believed in a more Darwinian approach.

5.4 Decentralized Autonomous Organizations (DAOs)

A Decentralized Autonomous Organization is a sophisticated smart contract. They have more code than other smart contracts because they govern more than just the transfer of value. DAOs have voting rights of members. The bylaws of DAO are in the code of the smart contract and are secured directly within their blockchain.

The concept of a DAO was created to address what in economics is referred to as the "principal-agent problem". The principal-agent problem is a dilemma that occurs when an "agent" can make decisions on behalf of another agent but is influenced by their own self-interest. The "agent" may choose to take more risk because they do not actually carry the cost of that risk. An example of this would be a CEO (the agent) who wants a short-term gain that nets them a bonus, rather than a longer-term choice that is better for the health and welfare of the company.

A DAO allows people to collaborate and agree on courses of action within agreed rules. The code within a DAO acts as the governance structure. For example, the DAO mentioned in the previous section was created to receive investment funds, and then safeguard them. Members of the fund could then vote on proposals that the community presented. Bylaws within the DAO set time frames for voting and, in general, establish the rules for how the funds would be managed, see figure 25.

The appeal of this new way of investing was that it allowed anyone with access to cryptocurrency to become a member of the investment group and vote on the investment projects. They didn't have to ask anyone's permission or make disclosures about their finances in the way that accredited investors have to within traditional systems.

Another appeal was that the code could not be amended and so criminal and unscrupulous individuals could not defraud the group. Only the members of the DAO could control it,

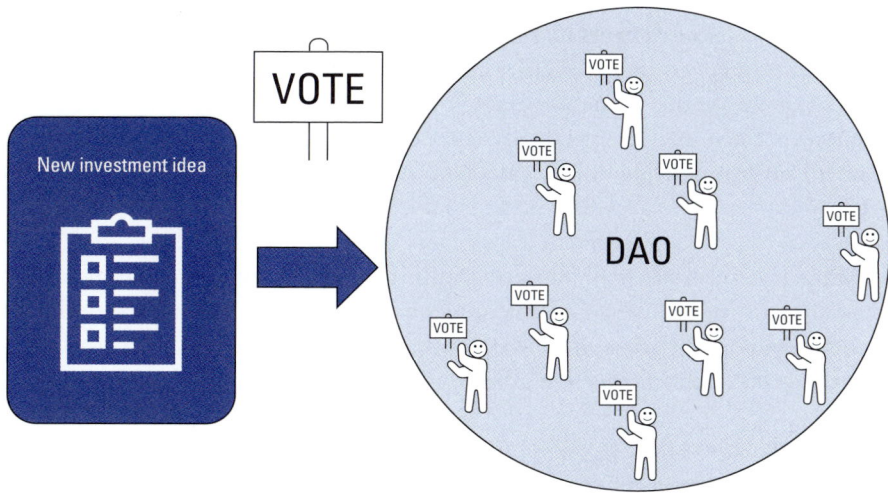

Figure 25   The owners of the DAO vote on proposals.

and each member's control was limited to what they had contributed. Members could leave and sell their membership in a marketplace. The DAO in effect removed the principal-agent problem.

Unfortunately, but perhaps not surprisingly, the code in the first DAO on Ethereum was not perfect. The imperfection was discovered quickly and exploited. One of the great strengths and weaknesses of open source code is that anyone can look at it and find ways to subvert what you are trying to do. A strength is that it can help you uncover bugs quickly, but sometimes at a high cost. Smart contracts that hold cryptocurrency or something else of value are vulnerable because their code is exposed to everyone and hackers are incentivized to break them.

The Bitcoin network is considered to be a DAO. It allows any person to join in the creation and security of the system and cooperation is completely voluntary. The rules for the network are held within its consensus protocol, and the miners vote by choosing what blocks to build on.

DAOs can now be used to do a lot more when applied to the idea of traditional organizations. For example, they could be used for voting for a new government, or by shareholders in a public or private corporation irrespective of the size.

DAOs hold a lot of potential in helping remove some of the less savory parts of business and politics and allowing individuals a fair voice in the things that they have invested in. Instead of the hierarchical structure that is employed by most governments, militaries, and corporations to manage all aspects of our society, a DAO presents a new option. An organization can now more easily be governed by rules that are enforced through code. They allow for cleaner group decision-making as each person's voice is only as loud as their contribution (or some other arbitrary rule the group has chosen). For example, DAO voting would allow the shareholders to select the positions of the board of directors and the employees, or even the election of new government officials. DAOs could be used to manage public resources and help overcome another economic term "the tragedy of the commons". The tragedy of the commons is where self-interest depletes or destroys a natural resource. As in the example above, a DAO could allow for a democratic consensus on how to use or preserve these resources.

These examples have extreme limitations within our current system. Judicial systems are still essential to justice and the enforcement of laws and the protection of physical property. However, within the borderless Wild West of the internet, these types of structures are intriguing as they may allow for further globalization.

How DAOs work

DAOs run through rules encoded within their smart contracts. They live completely online but can govern assets that are offline, like real estate or natural resources. DAOs allow two parties that have never met to cooperate and make decisions on a thing of value that they both share an interest in maintaining. DAOs enable these individuals to do things like hiring other individuals to perform tasks that can't be automated. Many DAOs have hired individuals to develop software, for example.

DAOs rely on tokens to gain cooperation. The tokens act as an internal property that has value and is controlled by the group. The group's actions are governed by the rules written into the DAO's smart contract. The tokens can represent shares that give voting rights, pay dividends, or are given out as rewards for cooperation.

Once you have deployed your DAO, it is autonomous. Many blockchains transition to autonomy slowly as small groups are more vulnerable to attack, at least within the context of public blockchains and mining. Public blockchains need to reach a critical mass of decentralization to withstand things like a mining pool being attacked. This is when a pool of miners will rotate quickly from one blockchain to another in order to optimize how quickly they can harvest and sell a cryptocurrency. These types of mine-and-dash activities can be damaging to the blockchain as it drives down the crypto prices and can leave the blockchain transactions stalled.

Key takeaways about DAOs

All of a DAO's transactions are a record within its blockchain. The transparency in accounting and financials lets the code act as the accepted, trusted third party.

DAOs gain consensus by having their members vote on important issues such as the withdrawal or movement of funds. A majority of its stakeholders specified in the smart contract must agree on all decisions. Many smart contracts give voting windows so that proposals and actions are not held up by non-responsive members.

A DAO cannot build a product or perform a service. They allow groups to organize and make decisions and then hire contractors to do things like writing code or developing a product. Contractors are selected by shareholders who vote.

Many DAOs depend on outside groups to generate proposals for things like the development of software. Some DAOs require financial deposits to prevent being inundated with proposals that are too general or of little or no value ("proposal spam").

All public blockchains are DAOs; these include Bitcoin, Ethereum, Factom, etc. DAOs can be more than public networks. They can be used to manage all types of human organizations such as corporations, investment funds, or even governments.

Legality of DAOs

The code and capabilities of DAOs do not absolve individuals from complying with regulations and laws. If you are thinking about creating a DAO, seek legal counsel.

Many countries have begun to create a legal framework that allows for the unique nature of DAOs. For example, Malta created a legal framework for DAOs that classifies them as a new type of legal entity, referring to them as "technology arrangements". Malta has created a new regulatory body called the Digital Innovation Authority (MDIA).

Many other countries including Estonia, Singapore, the United Kingdom, and more have been proactive in creating legal frameworks and regulatory sandboxes that allow entrepreneurs to explore new business models while staying firmly within the law.

5.5 Summary

Smart contracts and their many iterations such as DAO, ERC-20, and ERC-721s have all helped move blockchain technology from being more than simply a history of cryptocurrency transactions. They are the first use cases of blockchain technology that the average person can create themselves. This chapter has prepared you to understand the fast passed ICO (initial coin offerings), tokens, DApps, and the DAO market.

5.6 Test your knowledge

1. **What is a smart contract?**
    A. A type of token used for fundraising.
    B. The only application for blockchain technology.
    C. Programmers create smart contracts. They encode business logic into a self-executing program inside a blockchain.
    D. Lawyers create smart contracts. They encode business logic into a self-executing program inside a blockchain.

2. **Are smart contracts legally binding?**
   A. Yes
   B. No

3. **What enforces a smart contract?**
   A. Smart contracts are enforced by governments.
   B. Smart contracts are enforced by Bitcoin core development.
   C. Smart contracts are enforced with Boolean logic.
   D. Smart contracts are enforced with Boolean logic, mathematics, and encryption.

4. **What is a token?**
   A. Tokens are self-authenticating data packets and represent a rare digital bit of information.
   B. A non-fungible digital asset.
   C. A fungible digital asset.
   D. An ICO fundraising tool.

5. **Cryptocurrencies and tokens are the same things.**
   A. Yes
   B. No

6. **What is an ERC-721 token?**
   A. A common use for the ERC-721 is digital collectibles. It allows an issuer to prove uniqueness and transferability of a digital asset while allowing each asset to be unique.
   B. A common use for the ERC-721 is digital assets that are all the same.
   C. ERC-721 allows an issuer to prove uniqueness but can't be transferred.
   D. A common use for the ERC-721 is ICOs.

7. **What is an ERC-20 token?**
   A. ERC-20 tokens are non-fungible tokens and are commonly used for fundraising.
   B. ERC-20 tokens are fungible tokens and are commonly used for fundraising.
   C. ERC-20 tokens are fungible tokens and are commonly used for voting.
   D. ERC-20 tokens are fungible tokens and are commonly used for collectibles.

8. **What is a DApp?**
   A. DApps are decentralized applications that run on a central network.
   B. DApps are types of tokens that run on a P2P network instead of a single system.
   C. DApps are decentralized applications used to create tokens.
   D. DApps are decentralized applications that run on a P2P network instead of a single system.

9. **What is a DAO?**
   A. DAOs are Decentralized Autonomous Organizations and are sophisticated smart contracts that have things like voting rights of members.
   B. DAOs are only used for investment management.
   C. DAOs are simple smart contracts that have things like voting rights of members.
   D. DAOs are devolved independent groups and are sophisticated smart contracts that have things like voting rights of members.

10. **DAOs have legal standing.**
    A. Yes
    B. No

6 Expanding applications of blockchain

Blockchain has become more than just a buzz word, it has begun to reshape business models across many sectors. In this chapter, you will explore the ever-growing adoption of blockchain technology and learn how businesses will be affected by the new types of decentralized identity and why old marketing tactics may not work in the future.

You will uncover how AI (Artificial Intelligence) is using blockchain databases to secure information and buy data for training. This chapter also explores how IoT (Internet of Things) devices are securing themselves with distributed ledgers. Lastly you will learn about innovation in decentralized marketplaces and the effect these innovations may have on old business models.

Understanding how these technologies work together is essential because they are leading to changes in security, economies, and markets. The merger of these applications of blockchain is widespread and this chapter will give you a taste of what is to come in the next few years.

6.1 Decentralized identity

Blockchain technology is a distributed, unchangeable database that is autonomous and operates peer-to-peer. The "block" in blockchain contains a complete and accurate record of each transaction that has occurred on that blockchain, that cannot be changed once verified and is cryptographically secured. The linear, comprehensive, global, and secure characteristics of blockchain make it an excellent platform for securing all kinds of information. This includes for people, such as their identity documents, and for things, such as websites and data feeds from IoT devices.

In this section, you will uncover some of the defining features of this technology that make it an ideal place to secure the identities of people and things. You will see how peer-to-peer identities work and how they eliminate the need for intermediaries such as Yahoo or Equifax to hold on to your personal information. You will explore some of the new identity applications being built to solve a range of identity theft issues that affect businesses and people alike.

Online identity - the honey pot
The internet is more consolidated then you may realize. There is only a small group of companies that have control over issuing website security certificates and curating and cultivating online identities. This centralization has caused huge volumes of personal data to be housed on centralized servers for everyone who uses the internet. These servers can and do get hacked. With one place to target, the concentration of personal data by small groups of companies is a rich honey pot that will continue to attract similar data breaches like the ones that have targeted the FBI, Equifax, Target, Home Depot, Yahoo, and countless others.

Blockchain technology provides a potential solution to the problem of centralized data by enabling people and companies to store or secure data using a distributed blockchain database, rather than a central database that is more easily hacked. Information, once stored on a blockchain, is secured cryptographically and cannot be altered or deleted. Information is broken into smaller units thus making massive data breaches very difficult, if not theoretically impossible. Instead of everyone's data living in one place, each individual's data lives in its own highly secure environment. This data structure is already being explored by the U.S. Department of Homeland Security as a way to prevent data loss and spoofing of IoT devices such as cameras and ground sensors. Stealing or gaining control of data that is secured using this method means each targeted unit, whether it was a personal identity or the data feed from a connected device, would need to be hacked individually.

While storing data on a blockchain from a high level seems clear, there are multiple approaches that are being explored to actually implement it. One tactic is to eliminate the need for intermediaries by enabling you to store your identity documents and other relevant data directly on a blockchain. You would control your own information and be ultimately responsible for safeguarding and recovering it if lost. You would, theoretically, no longer need to provide sensitive data to any third party.

Using distributed ledger technology or blockchain technology, an individual is able to prove information without revealing supporting data. For example, your identity card contains lots of private information about who you are and where you live. This information is not needed for most interactions where you are asked for your identity. If you had a digital identity card that utilized blockchain technology, you could prove for example your eligibility to purchase alcohol without revealing your age or where you live, or even your name. Civic, a blockchain software start-up has created an age-verifying beer vending machine in partnership with Anheuser-Busch that does just that.

Another approach being explored by software companies is to encode your personal data onto a private and permissioned blockchain (known as a DLT) that can only be accessed by authorized third parties via a cryptographic signature from you. This approach does not eliminate the need for intermediaries but adds a layer of security and permission. It would eliminate the need for intermediaries to store sensitive personal data directly in one location. These types of systems would also empower you to know which individuals had looked up your information.

Blockchain technology can potentially eliminate the need for intermediaries and allow people total control over their digital identities, while others have suggested that companies can still process personal data but use blockchain technology to access and verify this data without using easily-hacked servers.

Self-sovereign identity
Blockchain protected and shared identity solutions have become a major development effort by the industry. Blockchain technology has allowed for a shift in the concepts of

Expanding applications of blockchain

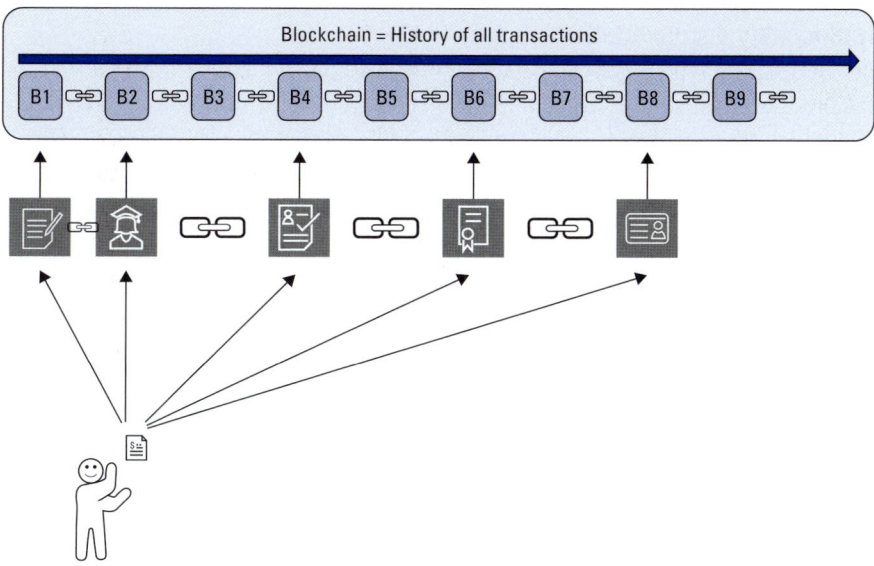

Figure 26 Blockchain protected identity – information about a person can be written into a blockchain using small transactions to create an unalterable history of what happened and when.

self-ownership. It has sparked new life into social movements around the moral and natural rights of each person to have exclusive control of their money, property, and identity.

A self-sovereign identity is one that is managed by an individual and not a third party. You would authenticate yourself and not rely on a third party to validate and corroborate your credentials. Within a blockchain system this can be accomplished by publishing cryptographic proof. The proof can have other information associated with it too. For example, you have created proof of a university certificate that confirms you have graduated. Your diploma can then be validated by another party, and they can publish a note that they checked and validated that "yes" you do have this credential at a given point in time.

What is identity?

Before we dive into how blockchains can be used to secure and create digital identities that are more robust then our current analog and centralized systems, it is useful to take a look at what "identity" is and how technology has affected identity over time.

Identity is a very broad term, and there are different definitions based on the context. For example, your identity may be a birth certificate, a government-issued driver's license, a social media profile, or the history of course work you have completed. For a device like a camera, it would be made up similarly. It would have been manufactured at a plant, shipped to a store, stored at a warehouse, and then eventually sold to you. Each of these moments in time is marked with documents and data. In the simplest terms, identity seeks to define who you are and what you have done over time. Entities such as the FBI, Equifax, Target, Home Depot and Yahoo all collect this information to try and understand more about you and the rest of the world so that they can improve on what they do.

History of identity documentation

The idea of defining who a person is has been in existence since time immemorial. Initially the main challenge was verifying the identity of a person in question as it depended on memory, which may, at times, fail. In countries like Algeria, South Africa, and Israel, the residents used beads more than 100,000 years ago to display their identity. You could know the family ties, personal identification, and wealth status when you studied these beads. Ancient Egyptians used tattooing as a form of creating and verifying identities. This practice dates back to 2000 B.C., and you could tell a person's clan, place in the society, and family members based on the tattoos they had.

Skin markings and physical symbols were later phased out as people developed record-keeping technologies and written language. In 3800 B.C., the Babylonians became the first known people to have a census by formally collecting all of their citizens' information.

King Henry V of England was the first person to introduce the idea of passports in 1414. English citizens would use these documents to prove their identities while in foreign countries. The British Parliament in 1829 passed legislation that allowed the government to come up with a database that could store the identity of its citizens. Other countries would follow suit and develop physical databases for recording the identity of their citizens. Germany, Czech Republic, Spain, and Singapore were the first countries to issue government smartcards in the 1980s.

In the early 1990s, online identities started to become prevalent with the popularization of online chat rooms. Your online identity was created through all the information you deposit online as you scroll Facebook, make a purchase online, or take a course through an online portal. Your internet browser collects all your online interactions and sums up your characteristics to define your online identity and target you for advertisements or even surveillance.

Every website builds a unique picture of who you are. These partial identities are aggregated by other businesses and sold. For instance, when you visit Amazon it creates an online identity based on the products you browse and buy. They then target you with products that you are more likely to want and buy. Google in a similar way is always trying to present you with relevant information, and they tailor what is displayed to you based on profiles that they develop. They create these profiles from the searches you make and your location.

These are all changing and growing pictures of who you are and how you change over time, but they are not legal, and many counties require companies to provide you with the information they collect on you and allow you to force them to delete it. The recent Cambridge Analytica scandal exposed that Facebook gathers between 4,000 and 10,000 data points on users that they then associate with that user's identity. These data points are collected over time and updated with the user's behavior. They create an incredible user profile and identity but are not legal to use in most countries for things like loan approvals.

Your legal identity comprises the documents that have been issued to you by a government, such as your birth certificate and driving license. They create a link between you and the region you are from and grant you protection and rights from that government. Most government agencies and organizations require people to have government-issued identification documents for them to access various services. The basic identity documents that almost all children get are birth certificates. Identity documents change from one jurisdiction to another. Some countries incorporate all the identities into a single card, whilst others have different cards such as identity cards, driving licenses, and social security numbers in various other documents.

Challenges of identity

It is clear that having an identity is crucial for identifying people and allowing others to have a level of trust. Identity allows us to know if someone is qualified for a job, able to pay, or whether it is safe to leave our children in their care. At a basic level, identity helps us trust one another and helps us to interact. Because identity is a short cut to trust, criminal groups target the documents and data that make them up. Our current systems have many challenges, which make it hard for governments and organizations to classify people and protect the information they store.

The number one issue is the security of online data. There is no assurance that the data some online organizations and governments collect to create identities is safe and will not be leaked or sold to third parties. Such databases are prone to hacks, and the identities of individuals end up in the hands of malicious people. Take, for instance, when you shop online through a platform that is not secured; hackers can tap your credit card details and later make purchases using your identity. It may take you years to recover from these types of theft and fraud.

Another issue that governments face, especially with porous borders, is identity verification. There is not a uniform way to name people, for example, and the differences in naming conventions cause interoperability problems. Every government has a different approach when it comes to creating the identity of its citizens. This is true for companies that manage user accounts. For instance, Amazon will be interested in your purchases and preferences, while Facebook's interest is on your social interaction. These two organizations will have different identities for the same person. Governments face the same problem; each country has a different system to create ID cards, passports, and birth certificates.

A third key issue is trust. Centralized systems can be compromised, and documents can be faked or changed, making it difficult to verify identities. Facebook hit the news headlines in 2018 after it shared the personal data of more than 87 million customers with Cambridge Analytica, which is a third party. That information was then used to manipulate individual's behavior. Convenience and ease of use has compromised many people's identities and financial information.

The final issue to note is that there is no way of proving that the data the user provides is true. Marketplaces have developed to sell user's profiles and personal data, enabling unscrupulous people to misrepresent themselves or fully take on another's identity, see figure 27. Governments and other organizations may not have access to data stored in other places, which means that it is hard to determine whether the data provided is the true identity of the person in question.

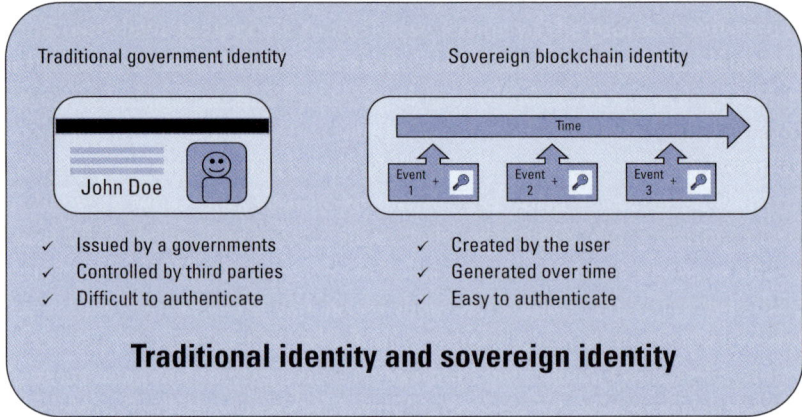

Figure 27   Traditional identity and sovereign identity.

6.2   Blockchain protected identity

Blockchain technology can eliminate the need for intermediaries and enable people to have full control over their digital identities and their legal identities too. Blockchain technology is being used to secure websites and connected hardware devices (IoT). In this section, you will see how businesses are building solutions to improve digital identity while still allowing all appropriate parties the access they need to private information.

Blockchain technology developers have promised to solve most of the challenges that governments, organizations, and individuals face while they are trying to assign, verify, and manage identities. These organizations have created decentralized identity platforms to provide a fool-proof database that stores historical data, which makes it easy to verify the identity or the authenticity of data. These systems ensure that only authorized individuals or parties have the ability to access or make changes to the database and some actually prevent any changes at all.

There are dozens of companies that are using blockchain for decentralized identity solutions. In this section, we will look at four distinct projects:
- Blockstack;
- Microsoft;
- IBM;
- Civic.

Blockstack

This is one of the earliest companies to provide a solution for the creation of decentralized identities. Blockstack was founded in 2013 and named initially Onename app. The focus of this company is to eliminate intermediaries that pose a security threat when creating and managing identities. The users of Blockstack have full control over their data, which lowers the chances of identity theft. Blockstack has a browser that runs decentralized apps, and their users can encrypt and store data on various devices.

Blockstack capitalizes on the internet's design flaw that forces users to resort to third parties to create and manage identities. Its browser allows people to create their identities directly and thus eliminates the need for third party platforms such as Google and Facebook to authenticate them.

Microsoft

As one of the largest software companies in the world, Microsoft took an early interest in blockchain technology. Microsoft's distributed ledger platform on Azure is being used to create identity management solutions for both people and things. Part of this effort is a partnership they have with the ID2020 Alliance. It is a global public-private partnership that is committed to helping the 1.1 billion people around the world who don't have a legal form of identity.

Microsoft is collaborating with other major organizations such as the Decentralized Identity Foundation (DIF) to provide solutions. The DIF is an organization focused on developing an open ecosystem for decentralized identity and ensuring interoperability between all participants. Microsoft will use the Identity Overlay Network Infrastructure, which can process tens of thousands of transactions per second. They hope to secure billions of people's identities and allow them to interact securely over an interoperable system that is built on open-source components and standards.

IBM's Trusted Identity

IBM, through its blockchain Trusted Identity solution, has created a decentralized approach to identity management that is powered by its distributed ledger. IBM has a hybrid public permissioned blockchain, and through it they create "verify credentials". The verified credentials system allows trusted issuing organizations to issue credentials to individuals. In turn, those people can hold and present credentials to other verifying organizations within the IBM ecosystem. The platform is based on top-ranking open standards and collaborates with the World Wide Web Consortium (W3C) and Decentralized Identity Foundation.

IBM is leveraging its System Z architecture and global IBM cloud to establish highly secure and available identities. IBM wants to transform KYC (Know Your Customer), the rules for verifying identities in banking and augment it with artificial intelligence. The company is fusing both decentralized identity and AI to improve global KYC. This platform is a heterogeneous network, which means that business owners will use their existing systems and still benefit from the approach.

Civic

Civic's initial coin offering sold US$33 million in tokens for its identification project during a public sale.

With those funds, Civic built a blockchain-based identity network which can connect firms and users. They offer three solutions for identity management. The first, known as the Secure Identity Platform (SIP), is a verified identity for multi-factor authentication on web and mobile apps and removes the need for usernames or passwords.

Civic also created a reusable KYC product that allows a user to scan and verify identity documents and satisfy KYC requirements for things like ICOs or other financial technology. It uses the Identity.com marketplace to validate personal information with blockchain attestations and store identity data locally on the user's mobile device.

The third product that they developed is a Secure Relationships Verification solution, for which they have rethought how to use and manage digital profiles. Within their system, organizations work with users to confirm their involvement before listing them on their websites. Once verified, users can reuse the same attestation for all the relationships they have online.

6.3 Blockchain and IoT

You may have heard of the term IoT (Internet of Things) but not know exactly what it means or how blockchain technology will shape it. IoT refers to all connected devices on the internet. These could be video cameras, smart watches, ground sensors, or the thermostat in your home. Connected devices are pervasive and collect a dizzying amount of information about us every day. With news of these devices being hijacked, one major question keeps emerging however, how secure is the information collected about you?

Consider the data you are creating. For example, your Wi-Fi-enabled security cameras know when you are home. Your smart TV collects a lot of information about you too. It may even have your financial information if it's connected to your Netflix or Amazon account. Your smartphone is the most significant personal data creator since it has all your personal and financial information. Self-driving cars, although not widespread yet, could pose a physical threat if hacked. All of these devices are vulnerable because they can be directly hacked. Their identity is secured in a central database, there is one password that manages multiple devices, and the data feeds can be spoofed, see figure 28. Spoofing, in general, is a fraudulent or malicious practice in which communication is sent from an unknown source disguised as a source known to the receiver. Spoofing can apply to phone calls, emails and websites, or can be more technical, such as a computer spoofing an IP address, a Domain Name System (DNS) server, etc. Spoofing can be used to gain access to a target's personal information, spread malware through infected links or attachments, bypass network access controls, or redistribute traffic to conduct a denial-of-service attack.

> **Spoofing**
>
> **What is spoofing?**
> When a person or program disguises themselves as a trusted entity. They falsify data to obtain an illegitimate advantage.
>
> **What is email spoofing?**
> The email appears to be from trusted senders and contains acachments or links that install malware.
>
> **What is IP address spoofing?**
> IP spoofing targets a network to gain unauthorized access to a system. Hackers send messages with a fake or "spoofed" IP address.
>
> **What is phone number spoofing?**
> A hacker tricks caller ID by spoofing the number displayed to the receiver.

Figure 28 Spoofing.

Blockchains and distributed ledgers offer a new solution to secure data from devices. They can be used to allow smart connected devices to buy and sell items autonomously. Blockchain technology does this by creating a secure means of directly authenticating IoT devices without a certification authority. It is the same model used by Bitcoin and another cryptocurrency to authenticate users and allow for the transfer of value between accounts.

IoT can utilize blockchain secured identity to prevent a spoofing attack where a malicious party impersonates another device to launch an attack to steal data or cause some other disorder. Some blockchain platforms, such as Factom, allow for the creation of identity chains that enable two or more devices to communicate directly without going through a third-party intermediary and in effect, make spoofing more cost prohibitive. These data chains can be used as storage or database backups.

Factom developed a model that allows users to synchronize multiple devices against a single system of authority. It then distributed proof of the data feed across other blockchain networks to create extremely redundant and censorship-resistant systems. The Factom identity chain, designed for each device, creates a permanent record and uses cryptography to secure the data, ensuring only validated devices receive access. As new devices are added, their identity records become part of the blockchain for permanent reference. Changes to a device configuration are registered and authenticated in the context of the blockchain validation model, ensuring that any falsified records can be caught and ignored.

There are many other companies developing new and exciting technologies that utilize blockchain to protect IoT devices. In this section, we will look in more detail at the work at Toyota and IBM.

Toyota
Toyota is always looking to improve its product and manufacturing processes. In particular it is exploring new technologies including DLT (distributed ledger technology) and

blockchains to improve its systems. The Toyota Research Institute is exploring the application of blockchain technology as a means of enabling driverless cars. The Institute is working with five different companies and the MIT Media Lab on this project.

The main focus of Toyota at the moment is on data sharing for every trip that an autonomous car makes. Toyota Research Institute is working to create autonomous vehicles that are reliable and safe and is exploring the storage of driver data in a blockchain. One of the best uses of this data will be in the insurance industry. The car's 100 or more sensors will collect information and store it on a blockchain, and this data can be used to quickly determine precisely what happened and when in the event of an incident or accident. The insurance companies will use this information to determine premium rates, which reduces fraud as it increases transparency and reduces misrepresentation.

IBM

IBM filed a patent for a system that can 'privatize and utilize' all the information gathered from self-driving vehicles through distributed ledger technology. The car will have a 'threshold distance', which is the distance within which the self-driving car will recognize and react to its immediate surroundings. The car will send the information to the IBM blockchain and this will be accessible to other cars within the network. Sharing the data enables them to make smart decisions.

6.4   Artificial Intelligence and blockchain

Before considering how blockchain technology is merging with AI, it is essential that you understand from a high level what Artificial Intelligence is now and how it may change over time. Essentially AI is a branch of computer science that simulates human intelligence in machines. Software is programmed to mimic the actions of humans and think like them. And now AI has moved more into self-discovery, where it is given a task and then works to find the best solution. Some of these projects have resulted in AI developing its own programming language and creating strategies that have never been used before to solve problems.

AI falls under two broad categories based on how the systems are constituted. There is Weak AI, sometimes referred to as Narrow AI, which is used for narrow, well-defined tasks. The other category that has just begun to emerge is General AI, sometimes referred to as Strong AI. This type of Artificial General Intelligence (AGI) can successfully perform any intellectual task that a human can.

Weak AI, as the name suggests, is simple and does not involve many tasks, see figure 29. These systems are designed to handle a specific task repetitively. A good example is Cortana on Microsoft Windows OS, Siri on Apple and Alexa on Amazon. These AI assistants all have narrow goals and are designed to answer questions that you pose to them.

Strong AI systems, known as Artificial General Intelligence, performs several varied tasks and functions and more closely resemble the human mind in their flexibility and ability to learn, as also shown in figure 29. These systems are often self-developed, with the software programming itself. Because humans are not doing the programing they are not always fully understood by their human creators. The AI is given data to train on, and then it programs itself to solve problems without the intervention of humans. Smart cars are one of the best applications of a strong AI system.

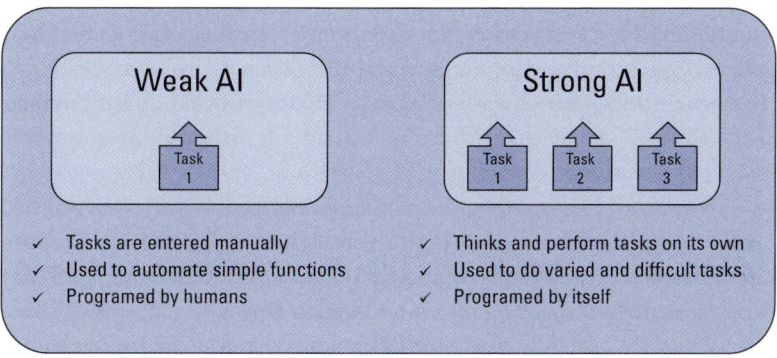

Figure 29   Weak AI versus strong AI.

Machine learning is one of the essential components of AI. A machine can study statistical models and algorithms that a computer system uses and then make an informed decision without human interaction. Machine learning improves time-based on the inputs that come on board and the interactions with the external environment.

The history of Artificial Intelligence

Humans had long since dreamt about using AI before they could create it. Ancient Greeks had myths about robots. Engineers in China and Egypt attempted to build and animate machines for more than a millennium. However, the term itself was not coined until 1956 at a conference held at Dartmouth College. It was the Dartmouth Summer Research Project on Artificial Intelligence held in the summer of 1956 that kicked off the field of AI.

Fast forward to today and there are many exciting opportunities to develop innovative applications utilizing a combination of blockchain and AI. . Blockchains create a secure and distributed ledger and public blockchains produce cryptocurrency. AI could benefit by conducting commerce anonymously, securing information globally, the data feeds that train AI could have a better reputation, and smart contracts could contain general AI.

Companies building blockchain technology for AI

In this sub-section, we will look further into the following startups' projects that are using a combination of AI and blockchain:
- SingularityNET;
- Enigma;
- Matrix AI Network.

SingularityNET

This platform is the brainchild of Hanson Robotics. It hit the headlines after making the first robot, Sophia, who is a citizen of Saudi Arabia. Robotics apply AI, and that explains why they get better with time and can make decisions based on the information they collect from the outside world. This platform was essential when developing features such as empathy, hearing, and sight capabilities for Sophia.

The main aim of SingularityNET is to decentralize the AI marketplace in order to make it easy to fund and develop AI systems. This marketplace has a network that is powered by AI algorithms that are sourced from all over the world. The marketplace is open, which makes it easy for developers and business owners to create AI projects through buying and selling AI data and algorithms. The platform draws its team from various players in the AI, machine learning, and blockchain fields.

Enigma

Enigma is creating an information marketplace that enables secure off-chain computing. It is often a dangerous and irreversible process to share information between parties. Someone who buys data could then widely distribute it, creating a free-rider problem. Enigma's new data marketplace called Catalyst allows organizations to contribute data which users can subscribe to and consume via smart contracts. The Catalyst market can be used by AI to facilitate training and building models.

Matrix AI network

Matrix AI is providing a solution that makes it easy to combine machine learning and smart contracts. The platform modifies how smart contracts are executed, and improves their speed, flexibility, ease and security. Matrix uses its mining power to solve expensive and complex AI computations.

The platform has several language options, which makes it easy for business owners to develop solutions in languages that they understand. It's part of China's major infrastructure projects, including the Belt and Road Initiative. The main aim of this project is to create an infrastructure that provides efficient and new land and sea routes that will facilitate transportation in different parts of the world.

6.5 Decentralized marketplaces and exchanges

A decentralized marketplace is a peer-to-peer platform that allows buyers and sellers to interact directly without involving a third party, such as Fruugo, PriceMinister, or Amazon. A decentralized marketplace does not have central control, and the data in this market is spread across many computers or devices through a blockchain.

A centralized marketplace is a platform with a central authority. They are often for-profit businesses that create a process which enables you to meet other buyers and sellers and complete transactions, but sometimes they can be facilitated by nonprofits. For instance, if you want to buy something from an online merchant such as Flipkart or Alibaba, the platform is the first intermediary, you will then have to deal with your payment gateway which is your bank and later the delivery company. Every intermediary gets a cut of the product that you bought, and you bear all the burden as the buyer, which makes the final product more expensive than if you had bought it directly from the manufacturer. On the other hand, a centralized marketplace will institute rules that you must follow and has the right to admit or ban you from the platform if you violate any of these rules.

Decentralized marketplaces have become more popular as users seek to retain control of their transaction. A decentralized market gives you control over your funds and the transaction, you as a buyer don't have to worry about your card details being stolen or receiving unexpected monthly charges. As a seller, you don't have to worry about fraud from stolen credit cards or chargebacks from customers. Decentralized markets are a bit of the "Wild West". There is a lot of trade of illicit items and fraud is still present. Anyone can come and buy and sell whatever they want.

Decentralized markets are not a new concept, people have been using them for long. A good example of such a marketplace is the foreign exchange market where people buy and sell currencies from all over the world. You do not need to visit a physical place to buy or sell currencies as you can do so over the internet where you can compare quotes from various dealers. The prices in a decentralized market depend on external factors such as economic times, inflation, political temperatures, and fuel prices. The introduction of blockchain to decentralized markets is making them more realistic and efficient. The first instance of merging the two ideas focused on trading cryptocurrencies, but it is quickly gaining traction in other markets as well.

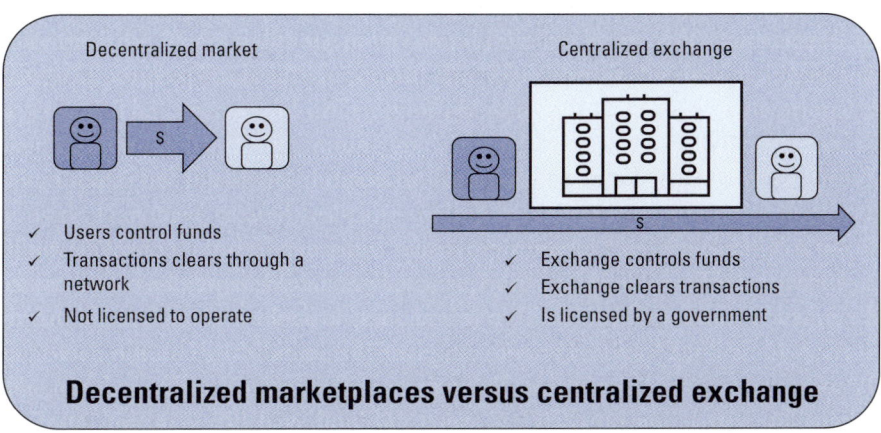

Figure 30 Decentralized marketplaces versus centralized exchange.

One of the blockchain's impacts, beyond cryptocurrency payments, for decentralized marketplaces is making them more tamperproof. They are resilient to being shut down and for better or worse can be accessed by anybody.

One of the main reasons that people use centralized marketplaces is due to the issue of trust. A blockchain decentralized marketplace solves this issue through smart contracts which come with preset conditions. Smart contracts self-execute once the conditions of the contract are met, which ensures that no one gets a deal that was not already pre-negotiated.

Challenges of decentralized marketplaces

A decentralized marketplace on the blockchain technology comes with a lot of benefits as indicated above. Some of the most outstanding include increasing transparency, ensuring a secure marketplace, reducing intermediaries, and protecting the privacy of the users. However, integrating the two concepts is not that easy due to the lack of legal enforcement and emerging developments.

Lack of legal framework

Governments and regional bodies are vital to protecting consumers. They help track down criminals who would harm consumers and commit fraud. Decentralized marketplaces are often black-marketed. Different governments are trying hard to come up with regulations on how to control decentralized markets, but it is not that easy. Anyone with some coding skills can create one and allow anyone in the world to post products and services for sale. They can build the market inside a blockchain network and make it difficult to take down or control.

Decentralized marketplaces use user reviews to help people navigate but they do not do enough when these reviews are easily faked. It is hard to trace people using a decentralized market because the user may be located anywhere in the world. However, there is a channel that allows law enforcement to control and track down bad actors. This is through the use of the cryptocurrency transaction to monitor the flow of capital on and off chain, since if users cash in or out of cryptocurrency they can be caught.

It should also be noted that decentralized markets are often used as loopholes for tax evasion.

Emerging developments

New technology is always slower and clunky at first and blockchain markets are no exception. A decentralized market uses a lot of different coding languages and consensus mechanisms, accepting different tokens. On GitHub, you can find more than 6,500 blockchain projects that are active, and all use different approaches.

New efforts have begun to help standardize some of the underlying technology that these market use. Initiatives like the Ethereum ERC-20 are great examples of token standardization that allows for greater interoperability. Groups like the Institute of Electrical and Electronics Engineers (IEEE) are working to create standards that allow for the development and adoption of blockchain technologies. Universities have begun to contribute too, for example Oxford, Stanford, and Berkeley all have blockchain initiatives.

Loss of customer touch

There is a reason why you head to your favorite shop every time. Most likely this is not only because of the quality of the products but the quality of the service as well. Receiving a personalized message from them might make you go back to the exchange. Centralized marketplaces focus significantly on the user experience, but you are unlikely to get much on a decentralized exchange. The developers in the latter are contributors, and they may not pay as much attention to the user interface.

Popular decentralized marketplaces and exchanges

There are many decentralized marketplaces and exchanges. It is even common now to see them built within cryptocurrency wallets, such as Waves. The following three are some of the more notable decentralized markets that are worth exploring:
- OpenBazaar;
- ModulTrade;
- FundRequest.

OpenBazaar

It is one of the oldest decentralized marketplaces and was originally known as Dark Market prior to 2014. You can open a free shop or e-commerce site on OpenBazaar and list your products. It does not charge a commission like other online merchants such as Amazon, Alibaba, and eBay, which means you can sell your goods at a lower price. You need to download a software script that acts as the web browser to use this marketplace.

Its differentiation is that it has an escrow service which holds the funds until the goods in question have been delivered. You do not need a credit card as you can pay for your goods using cryptocurrencies such as Bitcoin, Litecoin, and Ethereum.

ModulTrade

ModulTrade is a platform that helps small businesses compete fairly with big brands in the market. Most small-scale traders find it hard going beyond their borders, but ModulTrade wants to take them global. This platform has set up three steps to make the idea practical.

The buyer and the seller enter into a smart contract with some guidelines as the first step. The buyer then enters the funds into an escrow as the second step. Lastly, the seller will provide the products and ship them to the buyer. The smart contract will maintain tabs on the activities and will self-execute once all the conditions are met.

FundRequest

FundRequest marketplace is a platform for open-source software development. Software developers are a crucial part of the decentralized marketplaces and the blockchain field. As a business owner, you can request development for issues such as security audits and bug fixes or any other development work you may require. You interact one-to-one with the developers, explain your problems or requirements and you pay them to resolve these. Research shows that open-source software saves business owners US$60 billion per year.

FundRequest has some control measures to protect both the buyer and the developer. It has a native token known as FND. A developer has to stake some FNDs on the platform to ensure that he or she is committed to the job. Failure to complete the project as agreed will lead to loss of the stake. It ensures that developers do not take more jobs than they can handle at once.

6.6   Summary

This chapter has described how digital identity is being reshaped by both distributed ledgers and blockchain technology. Globalization and unrest have heightened the need to authenticate individuals quickly and accurately and allow people to have an identity that can't be destroyed due to natural disasters or war.

We have covered the AI revolution and the two broad types of AI development. In addition, we have looked at how individuals globally are conducting business without ever having met and without the support of a third party. These three changes are each unique ways in which one technology is reshaping the future of how we identify ourselves, conduct business and optimize systems. The way we create data, how we distribute data and then execute upon the data is changing.

6.7   Test your knowledge

1. **Personal identification information is stored online in databases that cannot be compromised.**
   A. Yes
   B. No

2. **How is identity data secured within a blockchain?**
   A. Data secured with a blockchain is bundled together with a hash and this helps to make massive data breaches very difficult.
   B. Data secured with a blockchain is broken into smaller units and published so everyone can read it.
   C. Data secured with a blockchain is locked into a smart contract and this makes massive data breaches very difficult.
   D. Data secured with a blockchain is broken into smaller units and this makes massive data breaches very difficult.

3. **What is self-sovereign identity?**
   A. A self-sovereign identity can't be lost or destroyed.
   B. A self-sovereign identity is published online by an NGO and is ideal for refugees.
   C. A self-sovereign identity is one that is managed by an individual and not a third party.
   D. A self-sovereign identity is one that is managed by a third party and not an individual.

4. **What is a legal identity?**
   A. Legal identities are the documents that have been issued to you by a government, such as birth certificates and drivers' licenses. They create a link between you and the region you are from and grant you protection and rights from that government.
   B. Legal identities are the documents that have been issued to you by private organizations. They create a link between you and the organization that grants you rights and privileges.
   C. Legal identities are stored online by a government and they create a link between you and the region you are from and grant you protection and rights from that government.
   D. A legal identity creates a link between you and the people in your family.

5. **What does IoT stand for?**
   A. Industrial Online Technology
   B. Internet of Things
   C. Industrial Organized Things
   D. Internet of Technology

6. **Why are IoT devices vulnerable?**
   A. IoT devices can be directly hacked because their identity is secured in a central database, there is one password that manages multiple devices, and the data feeds can be spoofed.
   B. IoT devices can be directly hacked because they only have one password often just "password" that manages multiple devices.
   C. IoT devices can be directly hacked because there is one password that manages multiple devices, and the data feeds can be spoofed.
   D. IoT devices can't be directly hacked because their identity is secured in a central database.

7. **What does AI stand for?**
   A. Artic Internet
   B. Armed Intelligence
   C. Arbitrary Intellect
   D. Artificial Intelligence

8. **What are the two types of AI?**
   A. Broad AI that can do anything a human can and Singular AI that is focused on one task.
   B. Narrow AI and Super AI.
   C. Machine learning and Narrow AI.
   D. Weak AI or sometimes referred to as Narrow AI. It is used for narrow, well-defined tasks. The other category is General AI or sometimes referred to as Strong AI that preforms multiple tasks.

9. **What is a decentralized marketplace?**
   A. A decentralized marketplace is a peer-to-peer platform that allows buyers and sellers to interact directly without involving a third party.
   B. A decentralized marketplace is a platform that allows buyers and sellers to trade goods and services, like Amazon or Alibaba.
   C. A decentralized marketplace is an open platform that allows you to buy and sell anything you want.
   D. A decentralized marketplace is an open platform that allows buyers and sellers to interact directly and uses a third party to resolve disputes.

10. **What are three popular decentralized exchanges?**
    A. Amazon, ModulTrade, FundRequest
    B. Ripple, Ethereum, Bitcoin
    C. OpenBazaar, ModulTrade, FundRequest
    D. Apple, Amazon, Alibaba

7 Blockchain and the world economy

The world economy has become more connected every year and globalization has changed the lives of people and communities significantly. The fast-paced changes in technology and the increased mobility of commodities, money, and people have strained our current systems considerably. Blockchain technology is one of the many innovations that both enables new levels of globalization and helps some of our existing institutions reinvent themselves.

Our interdependence, though in many ways straining, has grown the world GDP from approximately US$50 trillion in 2000 to over US$80 trillion in 2017. It is crucial to analyze the current systems as well as emerging trends to devise business and political solutions that can address these challenges.

Blockchain technology has many ways to augment and add efficiency to a number of the critical systems that power globalization. In this section, you will learn more about the challenges that supply chains, cross-border payments, digital fiat currency, and insurance all face and how blockchain technology is currently being applied.

7.1 Supply chain industry

A supply chain is a network between a company and its suppliers who produce and distribute a product. The entire industry is mostly composed of independent for-profit companies, all engaged in the production and delivery of products. The network works collaboratively and in our globalized world this means that the coordination of raw materials, parts, assembly, shipment, and hundreds of actions occur across the globe. These global networks rely heavily on record keeping systems and the ability to securely and accurately share information with relevant parties.

The supply chain market in the U.S. was previously valued as US$13 billion in 2016, and is expected to exceed up to US$19 billion by 2021. The supply chain analytics market in the US, which focuses on the use of big data and predictive analysis, is a supply chain segment valued at US$3.05 billion by 2017, and is expected to reach over US$9.88 billion by 2025. The supply chain management market in the U.S. on the other hand, which involves the management of the flow of goods and services, was valued at US$12.96 billion in 2017, and is expected to grow up to US$30.6 billion in 2026.

The growth across the sector has increased competition and the need to create efficiencies wherever possible. Blockchain technology and its ability to create a globally accessible record that can be collaborated on by multiple stakeholders has a tremendous amount of potential. Another aspect of blockchain technology, separate from the collaborative record-keeping functionality, is the ability to transfer value, or tokenized ownership through just a software system.

Supply chain of the past

The invention of supply chains dates back to prehistoric times, growing from one group of people needing to trade with another. The transportation of goods was difficult, dangerous, and costly for most of human history. Warehouses, one of the earlier supply chain innovation, were built to help protect assets, reduce costs, and stabilize supply and prices. They were strategically placed near sources of the raw materials and the production of the goods.

These linear networks of suppliers, warehouses, and transportation services between trade hubs were further strengthened with the establishment of trade routes. The Silk Road between China and Europa, through Central Asia and the Spice Route in the Indian Ocean are both still known today.

The Industrial Revolution occurred because of breakthroughs in the systemization of manufacturing and production. All the new products demanded improvements in transportation technology, including railways, shipping (including steam ships) and roads.

The birth of telecommunications was a game changer. It allowed suppliers, manufacturers, shippers and buyers to communicate nearly instantly where it had once taken days or weeks. It enabled more efficient communications in the supply chain revolution. Combined with containerization, where products are stacked and stored together and delivered at a later time to save costs, the supply chains became more efficient, cheaper, and faster. There still is disparity in the technology and abilities at each of these levels in the supply chain. However, as the cost of smart phones and other digital devices continue to plummet, clipboards and paper bills of lading will be replaced with digital versions.

Supply chain of the future

Several anticipated trends are expected to affect the supply chain industry in the next few years. Laws, treaties and trade agreements, for instance, can change supply chains both politically and geographically. Economic sanctions prevent the entry of cargo freights and ships, disrupting the supply chain network, and in doing so creating economic dead zones and poverty.

Further, free trade agreements allowing participating countries to trade freely, whilst imposing sanctions on non-participants, affect the network as well. These agreements and sanctions significantly impact how supply chain networks work, and may potentially disrupt the supply chain industry as a whole. This may sound destructive to markets but these measurements are necessary to help stem the flow of illicit goods, reduce human slavery, and protect intellectual property.

At this moment, supply changes are again going through a new revolution in technology. The automation of all aspects of the process is occurring now. Walmart is one of the world's most powerful suppliers and controls a vast global network. It has begun to automate the record keeping systems that allow it to know exactly where it obtains each item it sells. On the surface, this sounds easy, but with a global network of contractors, who subcontract portions of production, it becomes challenging to ascertain the exact origins of some products. Walmart, through a successful pilot project, can now trace the source of over 25 products from five different suppliers. It implemented private and permissioned blockchain technology from the Hyperledger Foundation. The company plans to roll out the system to more products and categories soon. Walmart has since announced that it will start requiring all of its suppliers of fresh leafy greens to trace its products using its blockchain.

NFC (Near-Field Communication) and RFID (Radio Frequency IDentification) are both forms of wireless communication that have created significant efficiency in warehousing, shipping and accounting by allowing companies to automate the identification and tracking of goods. These technologies have been paired with blockchain record keeping systems to again automate another layer of the supply chain, namely the recording of where items are at all times, who has ownership of them and when. Smartrac, the world's largest manufacturer of NFC and RFID tags, has launched an integrated document verification and authentication solution. The solution utilizes its IoT enablement platform, Smart Cosmos, its NFC transponders, and the Factom blockchain technology. These tags can be used for things like parts, raw materials, and documents. It hopes to create efficiencies in tracking and reduce fraud within supply chains.

Supply chain using blockchain technology

There are many startups in the supply chain industry that are using blockchain technology to increase efficiency and automation, and reduce fraud. In this section, you will learn more about three innovative companies:
- Everledger;
- OpenPort;
- ShipChain.

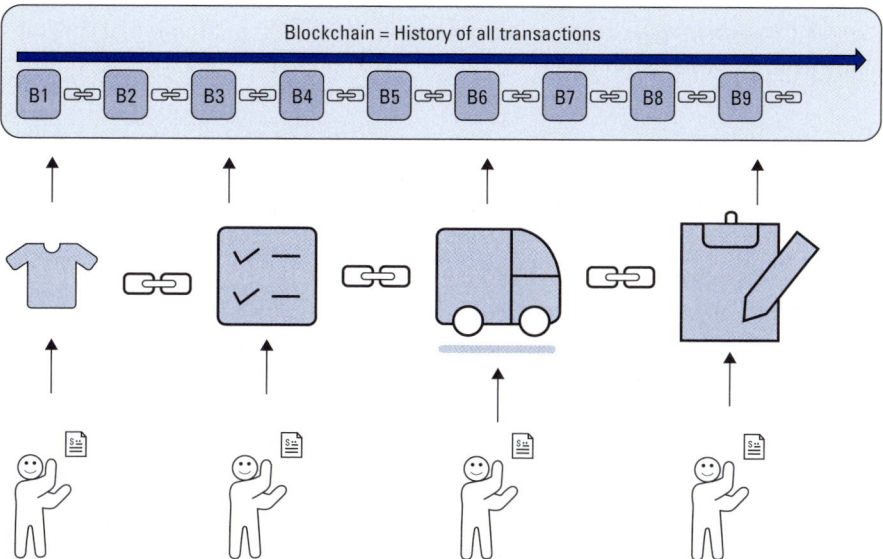

Figure 31 Supply chain - entries can be made to build a history of an item over time by multiple parties.

Everledger

Everledger is one of the earlier startups in the blockchain space that has been working on supply chain management. It creates a sharable history of ownership as a product is bought and sold. The ownership chain allows users to authenticate if a product has been ethically sourced and is genuine.

Everledger is particularly useful for goods like diamonds that are difficult to track. But with more and more scandals around the authenticity of food and wine it could help consumers purchase items that have a clear history of who contributed what. In cases where an item is found to be fraudulent or to contain a component that has an issue, it would be very easy to establish fault.

OpenPort

OpenPort is another emerging company in the supply chain industry that offers a solution to risk management. Using blockchain, it offers a digital approach to issuance which they call proof of delivery, to ensure cash flow and tracking are transmitted in real time. It offers an efficient approach to transactions using digital payment with cryptocurrency and helps create smart contacts, enabling faster and more efficient processing of delivery and operations.

As mentioned above, OpenPort's application generally focuses on real-time processes. This includes the efficient tracking of goods and the creation of a transparent and direct relationship between shippers and transporters. This will allow transporters and shippers to have direct communications on any specific requirement that the products being shipped may need.

Also mentioned is the use of its own digital currency, the OpenPort's Token (OPN). Using this token will allow the creation of a smart contract between the shipper and the transporter, making processes easier and faster.

OpenPort aims to maximize the power of technology by eliminating the use of paper trails through ePOD or Electronic Proof of Delivery. This will help speed up the transaction process, ensuring supply chain operations flow smoothly.

ShipChain

ShipChain focuses on shipment tracking and delivery, providing a fully integrated system for the supply chain industry through the use of transparent blockchain contracts to help track and trace the current location and status of every shipment and product in transit. This unique offering of visibility allows consumers to track where their products are, and at the same time rest assured that their privacy remains secure.

ShipChain offers three main services: Visibility, Trust, and Control. The main goal of ShipChain is to provide visibility for consumers to track their shipments and consolidate all these in a single platform. ShipChain uses blockchain technology to draft smart contracts, ensuring tamper-proof data to its consumers. Most importantly, ShipChain allows consumers to control their own data, permitting and restricting its release according to how they see fit.

7.2 Cross-border money transfer

Cross-border money transfer, better known as a remittance, is a type of funds transfer service done electronically by moving money from one bank to another, where the beneficiary of the funds resides outside the payee's country. It is a fast-growing competitive industry, with a compound annual growth rate of 10.4%. According to the World Bank, individuals globally sent each other US$580 billion in 2017, and this number is expected to grow to US$750 billion by 2023.

There are two general types of cross-border money transfers, depending on the bank that is managing the funds and the type of transfer that a consumer would like to perform. The cross-border direct inter-bank transfer refers to the type of transaction in which both of the banks where fund transfers are taking place hold an account in the other bank, and with the use of SWIFT (Society for Worldwide Interbank Financial Telecommunication) as a medium, accounts are credited accordingly.

The cross-border indirect inter-bank transfers are the second type of remittance, where neither of the banks have accounts with the other bank, and a third party must stand in between as the communication and intermediary line between the two banks for the transaction to take place. In this case, SWIFT will be responsible for looking for a bank in which both of the transacting banks have accounts in and will do the transactions from there. Notice that compared to the direct inter-bank transfers, indirect inter-banking has another layer of communication and provider, and thus it usually takes longer to complete the process.

A little history in cross-border money transfer

Person-to-person transactions started through a barter system during 300– 600 BCE, where traders would exchange silver, gold, and other precious stones in exchange for goods such as spices, wool, silk, wine, and the same.

The earliest coins, made of silver and gold, were first known to be in circulation around 610-600 BCE. Turkey, known back then as Lydia, would use this as its national currency, and people would use this as a means of exchange.

During the 15th century, the Italian Medici family opened several banks at foreign locations to provide foreign currencies. They are most famous for having introduced double entry accounting. Double entry accounting was a revolution in auditing and accounting. It allowed business and banks to balance their accounts more accurately and paved the way for the accumulation of great wealth. Blockchain is also seen as a revolution in accounting. Blockchain-backed asset are self-authenticating and clear and are settled on a distributed ledger.

You can think of this as triple entry accounting. They always balance, preventing fraudulent and counterfeit assets from being circulated or accepted.

The German merchant family, Fugger, were prominent bankers who took power after the Medici family. They controlled a significant portion of the European economy through trade with the East, their mining operations, and banking. They were the richest and one of the most powerful families in history and reiterated the lesson that those who take advantage of innovations, such as double-entry accounting, can accumulate vast fortunes.

During the 17th to the 18th century, Amsterdam worked on maintaining an active Forex Market, all done in the interests of England and Holland. In the late 18th Century, the U.S. adopted the dollar, and this is now best-recognized currency in the world.

Innovation in cross-border payment

In the middle of the 19th century Western Union was founded and they launched the wire transfer. This process uses electronic funds transfer from one person or entity to another through its telegraph network, effectively helping to move money within and across borders. Western Union still handles the majority of personal remittances globally.

By the late 20th century, the global network for the Society of Worldwide Interbank Financial Telecommunication (SWIFT) became the entity responsible for most international payments. Although it does not move money, the network facilitates the transmission of messages between banks, effectively allowing banks to get in direct communication to make the international money transfer process easier.

By the end of the 20th century, PayPal transformed the movement of money yet again. It utilizes the Barclays payment rails to enable online money transfer. This allows individuals to pay for products and services online with confidence and has been instrumental in transforming the internet from a passive and informational experience to an actionable one.

Cross-border payment of the future

Blockchain technology is now transforming the movement of money again. The Monetary Authority of Singapore partnered with blockchain company R3 and conducted the first inter-bank payments using blockchain technology in 2016. The project showed that banks could transact and settle round-the-clock and were no longer limited by time zones and office hours.

Nearly instant global 24-7 money transfer is possible because the record of value is self-authenticating. You may find it helpful to think about it like this. If for example, you are holding a dollar, then you know it is in your possession, and it can only be taken from you by force. In effect, a paper dollar is a bearer instrument. A bearer instrument entitles the holder to all rights of ownership. Cryptocurrency and tokens are digital equivalents for a bearer instrument, and they can prove their authenticity.

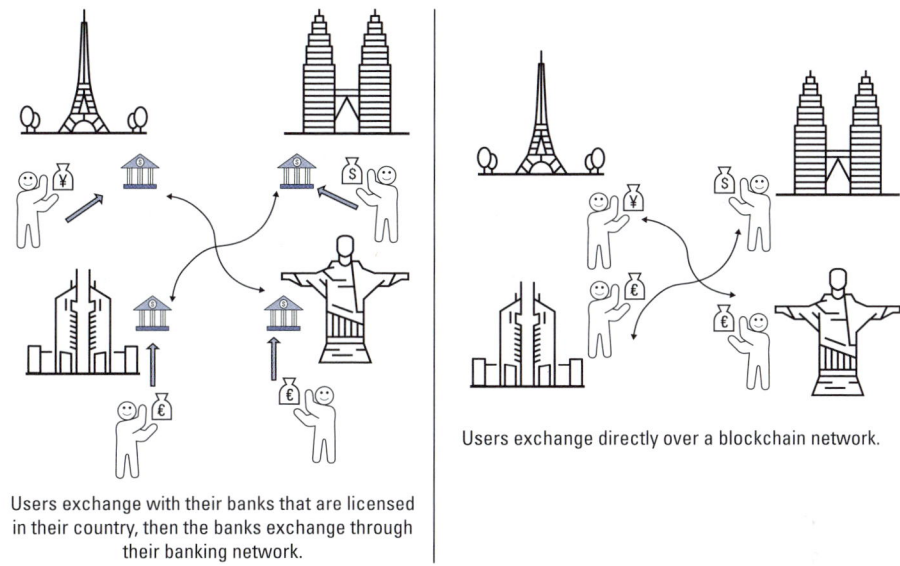

Figure 32   Cross-border payment: banking system versus blockchain system.

One of the key issues that cryptocurrency has faced has been around authority and legitimacy. Traditionally governments control the right to create money, and they allow banks to facilitate that service to the public. Cryptocurrency is a grassroots citizen creation, and many governments have rejected it. However, the technology introduces many new features that can help reduce costs in accounting and fraud. Central banks have taken quite a bit of interest in this, and in 2019 the central banks of Singapore and Canada sent each other digital currency via their private blockchain and without a third party.

The Monetary Authority of Singapore (MAS) sent funds to the Bank of Canada (BoC) by linking their two independent distributed ledgers (private blockchains), called Ubin (Singapore) and Jasper (Canada). They hope to expand the network to include more central banks' private blockchains and thus cut cost and increase efficiency.

Top three challenges in cross-border money transfer

There are different challenges in the cross-border money transfer industry. The three top most noteworthy challenges are high cost, constantly changing exchange rates and fraud.

Transaction processes for remittances is generally expensive. According to the World Bank the average cost to senders of remittances was 7.21%. This price is going down but is still linked to unstable changes in foreign exchange (Forex). Remittance centers and banks take a percentage of the amount as payment for processing. Banks using blockchain technology can have near-instant clearing and settling. Consequently, fluctuations in Forex become less of a problem and the costs per transaction on a private blockchain are negligible.

As mentioned earlier, exchange rates change every day and are dependent on the status of the country's economic state. Rates differ daily, and sometimes even hourly. This unstable state means the rate changes between the time you initiate a transaction in one country, and it is received and executed in the other country. Blockchain technology has introduced another solution to this issue beyond moving money faster. It allows for what is known as a stable coin.

Stable coins are different from cryptocurrency. They are a token that represents a fiat currency. A fiat currency is any legal tender that is backed by a government. If you remember in the example earlier that a paper dollar - known as fiat currency - is a bearer instrument and it entitles the holder all rights of ownership. The meaningful difference, beyond some technical structure, between a stable coin and the work done by the central banks is that normal people can hold stable coins, whereas only known members can read and write to their blockchain networks.

Fraud is a key issue and cost driver in cross-border payments. The American Payments Fraud & Control Survey found that wire transfer fraud has now surpassed credit and debit card fraud. It is making a real difference to companies, with 64% of businesses affected, and the rate has skyrocketed since 2014. The trend was driven by an epidemic surge in imposter fraud, fed by large scale data breaches such as the Equifax hack that exposed over 143 million U.S. citizens' personal information. Hacks are making the traditional credentials that people used to identify themselves less secure and reliable, as they are now globally public. Phones number and emails can be easily compromised. Again, blockchain may have some interesting solutions which allow an individual to utilize an identity that has chronology and provenance.

7.3 Financial change agents

Many blockchain technology companies have been working hard to gain market share in the remittance sector. In this section, you will learn more about key companies and what they are doing to revolutionize banking technology.

The Ripple protocol
Ripple, originating from Canada, has now grown to be one of the most influential leaders in financial technology. Its blockchain, that resembles a combination of both public and private blockchain technology, allows for two critical functions. It is:
- A common ledger that banks can use to settle payments globally;
- A neutral transaction protocol to trade things of value that do not have a well-formed market.

The main services that Ripple offers are:
- Real-time payments;
- Comprehensive transaction traceability;
- Near-instant reconciliation;
- The ability to convert almost any type of currency, commodity, or token.

The R3 consortium
R3 is a New York-based blockchain development company that started as a consortium of banks looking to create standards in financial technology and blockchain. They have since grown into one of the most important blockchain development companies in the world. They have designed and piloted many of the blockchain initiatives within banks and insurance companies.

R3's blockchain protocol is called Corda. It is a distributed-ledger platform designed to manage and synchronize financial agreements between regulated financial institutions. This means it is private and does not utilize a cryptocurrency. Key characteristics of Corda include:
- Controlled access, only designated parties can see data;
- There is no central party in control;
- It is regulatory compliant and oversight ready;
- Transactions can only be validated by authorized validators;
- It supports many consensus mechanisms;
- It has no cryptocurrency.

COTI
COTI is a blockchain platform offering a power grid of payments. It is a FinTech company offering a platform and payment solution by providing digital currencies. Using blockchain technology, COTI aims to provide a scalable and secure way of processing transactions using its platform.

COTI has developed a revolutionary way to help make remittance processing easier through its platform. It aims to provide a cheap, instant, smooth and frictionless way for carrying out all cross-border money transfers.

Apart from remittance technologies, COTI also offers various products such as a white label payment network, loyalty networks, stable coins, and COTI pay.

Everex
Everex is involved in the development of smart contracts and stable coins to support the digital currency initiatives of commercial and central banks. Instead of the tokens and cryptocurrencies, smart contracts are being used with blockchain technology for transactions.

Everex offers a wallet through its application, allowing digital fiat currency and asset tokens in exchange for fiat deposits in multiple currencies. It provides an option to send money and make payments in different currencies and digital assets to anyone including yourself. Everex offers different fiat currencies either through ATM, bank account, or cash pickup.

SendFriend

SendFriend is an application that offers a useful means of reducing the costs and improving the experience associated with sending remittances. As an example, this application caters more specifically for overseas Filipino workers to send money to support their families. SendFriend generally uses low fees to make payments easier for Filipinos, and money is usually sent online and ready for pickup in a few minutes. Most importantly of all, it offers a safe and secure application through its cutting-edge technology.

7.4 Summary

Supply chains and the payment for goods and services has become more interconnected and dependent every year. Blockchain technology and distributed ledgers are a possible solution to help ease some of the tensions of globalization. They allow people access to increased mobility of commodities and money while lowering costs and creating greater transparency.

This chapter has given you a broad overview of how our current systems for moving both things and money works. You have uncovered the interconnected network that allows a supply chain's producers of raw materials, manufacturers, suppliers, and other producers to create and distribute a product. You have learned how the SWIFT network has allowed banks to communicate. You have discovered the two types of cross-border money transfer; the cross-border direct inter-bank transfer and the indirect inter-bank transfer.

Blockchain technology and DLT are augmenting and adding efficiency to many of the critical systems that empower globalization. Now you have a better understanding of how companies and banks are using transparent records that help to reduce fraud. You have also discovered how banks and companies are taking advantage of self-clearing and settling assets.

7.5 Test your knowledge

1. **What is a supply chain?**
   A. A supply chain is a blockchain network companies use to buy and sell goods globally.
   B. A supply chain is a network between governments that traces ownership records of suppliers who produce and distribute a product.
   C. A supply chain is a network between a company and its suppliers who produce and distribute a product.
   D. A supply chain allows users to understand how the product they own was created. It shows the connection between suppliers and manufactures who produce and distribute a product.

2. **How is blockchain technology used within a supply chain?**
   A. Blockchains create a globally accessible record that can be collaborated on by multiple stakeholders.
   B. Blockchains create private records that can be collaborated on by multiple stakeholders.
   C. Blockchains create a globally accessible record that can be viewed by anyone at any time.
   D. Distributed ledgers create a globally accessible record that can be collaborated on by everyone in a supply chain.

3. **What is remittance?**
   A. A remittance is the communication about money between two banks that are not linked in a network like SWIFT.
   B. A remittance is the transfer of money where the beneficiary of the funds resides outside the payee's country.
   C. A remittance is when a bank pays a fine for allowing a customer to launder money.
   D. A remittance is a type of blockchain technology that allows for direct transfer of funds between two parties.

4. **What are the two types of remittance?**
   A. The rose border direct inter-bank transfer and the cross inter-bank transfer.
   B. The direct inter-bank transfer and the indirect inter-bank transfer.
   C. The direct inter-bank transfer and the non-inter-bank transfer.
   D. The cross-border direct inter-bank transfer and the indirect inter-bank transfer.

5. **What does SWIFT stand for?**
   A. Society for Worldwide Interbank Fiscal Telecommunication.
   B. Safer Communication for Worldwide Interbank Fiscal Communication.
   C. Society for Worldwide Interbank Financial Telecommunication.
   D. Society for Wider Interconnectable Fiscal Telecommunication.

6. **What does SWIFT do?**
   A. It is a network that facilitates the transmission of messages between banks. SWIFT allows banks to communicate directly and makes the international money transfer process easier.
   B. SWIFT is a consortium of banks that have collaborated on a blockchain network that facilitates the transmission of messages between banks. SWIFT allows banks to communicate directly and makes the international money transfer process easier.
   C. It is a bank that hold money for other banks. SWIFT allows banks to communicate directly and makes the international money transfer process easier.
   D. It is a network that facilitates the direct movement of money between banks. SWIFT allows banks to send each other money and makes the international money transfer process easier.

7. **Does SWIFT transfer physical money?**
   A. Yes
   B. No

8. **Why is remittance challenging?**
   A. Remittance is free, has no exposure to fluctuating exchange rates, and is not a target for fraud.
   B. Remittance is difficult because governments impose strong restrictions on money transfer such as AML (Anti Money Laundering) and KYC (Know Your Customer) that token and cryptocurrency users are not exposed to.
   C. Remittance has a high cost, is exposed to fluctuating exchange rates and is a target for fraud.
   D. Remittance is already fast, cheap, and easy. Blockchain technology offers no advantage for banks.

9. **When a cryptocurrency or token is used for cross-border transfer does it transfer ownership?**
   A. Yes
   B. No

10. **How does blockchain technology lower the cost of remittance?**
    A. Blockchains like SWIFT are a messaging platform for banks. They help banks communicate even faster.
    B. Blockchain creates an efficient central database for banks to check ownership records. Tokens and cryptocurrencies can help reduce some types of fraud and money laundering as they create a clear history of ownership.
    C. Tokens and cryptocurrencies do not reduce the time a user is exposed to fluctuating exchange rates. And they increase fraud and money laundering as there is no clear history of ownership.
    D. Tokens and cryptocurrencies are self-authenticating and can settle nearly instantly. They reduce the time a user is exposed to fluctuating exchange rates. Tokens and cryptocurrencies can help reduce some types of fraud and money laundering as they create a clear history of ownership.

8 New frontiers in blockchain and business

This chapter focuses on three industries that are being reshaped by blockchain technology. The first section uncovers digital fiat currency. Blockchain technology allows us to have trustless transactions both online and offline. Now banks and governments are looking to adopt this technology to improve their monetary systems. Insurance companies are looking to improve their operations and implement trustless transactions and smart contracts. They hope to lower costs and improve their customers' experiences. You will also learn about how individuals and companies are securing their intellectual property with blockchain technology and sharing their ideas and plans using an online environment.

These three industries all hope to utilize a distributed system to improve the sharing of information of value. The knowledge in this chapter is essential because it will give you the insights you need in three major industries that affect you and business daily.

After reading this chapter you will be prepared for the changes in how money works globally. You will understand how insurance companies will establish important events such as "who did what when" and automate that discovery process through IoT devices. You will gain insights into new trends in global intellectual property rights and the providence on information and physical goods.

8.1 Digital fiat currency

Central Bank Digital Currency (CBDC), more commonly known as the digital fiat currency, is defined as the representation in the digital form of a fiat currency of a particular nation (or region) and is issued and regulated by the competent monetary authority of the country.

A digital fiat currency acts as a digital representation of the country's fiat currency, which will be backed by financial reserves in the country such as forex and gold. It is designed in a way that the currency may be issued by private banks or the central bank, it is redeemable on demand and it clears nearly instantly. Consumers with no bank accounts will still be able to hold deposits, this time with their country's central bank, and will yield a different interest rate as compared to that of private banks. This will allow everyone to be able to save money and conduct transactions, even without traditional individual bank accounts.

Central banks are exploring the concept of digital fiat currency, both centralized options like eCurrency, private DLT networks such as Fnality, and blockchain-enabled projects such as Liquid by Blockstream. Each of these approaches structures the units of digital fiat slightly differently, but the concept is similar to blockchain cryptocurrencies and tokens in that the units are self-authenticating, preventing counterfeit, and are digital bearer instruments, clearing and settling between banks without trust and nearly instantaneously. Digital fiat currency will open easier means for people and businesses to conduct transactions electronically and globally as it has some of the best characteristics of cryptocurrencies while having the authority of a central bank.

History of digital fiat currency

Digital fiat currency is a new concept in the FinTech industry. Using electronics and technology as a means of financial transaction is a concept that the world is recently learning to adapt to, although it has prompted debates on its viability as the money of the future. Proposals leading to the possibility of using digital fiat currencies as a valid means of transaction, however, was developed due to central banks' needs to create safe, liquid instruments that the general public were able to use and primarily as a way of settling transfers of money between central banks. This is called "interbank settlement". Globally, many people are already conducting most of their transactions electronically and may not feel much of a difference in the way they buy or accept payments.

Another motivation for promoting digital fiat currency is the economic approach, especially in emerging economies, in which they will be able to cut the costs of printing and minting coins as well as managing physical money production as a whole. This, in turn, will help prevent issues such as counterfeiting and money laundering. It also provides a logistical solution for the general public, as the need to carry physical paper during travels decreases.

Digital fiat currency promotes digitization and adaption to better technologies. Not everyone has access to commercial banks, and so not everyone at present has the capacity to maximize the benefits of this electronic instrument. Promoting digital fiat currency will compel countries to improve their technology, allowing broader access to electronic money to more impoverished regions. The price of technology to manage both identity and cryptocurrency has been driven down so far, that it is now feasible for everyone, even in the poorest regions, to have a smartphone. The penetration rates for smart phones has hit an average of 82% in developing nations (Source: Deloitte, Global mobile consumer trends, 2nd edition, 2017).

Digital fiat, much like other blockchain innovations, removes the need for many intermediaries, including traditional banks. In order to remain relevant, they will need to offer additional services besides keeping funds safe. Credit and investment products will need to take center stage, as each individual globally may be able to act as their own bank, holding their money and sending transaction without interacting with a bank.

Digital fiat currency could be used as a tool to stabilize failing economies and countries. For example, a central bank could push funds directly to digital wallet holders within minutes, giving individuals money and fueling the economy. Initial coin offering took advantage of the concept of an "airdrop" to send their tokens to digital wallets. These airdrops would kickstart a new project and help it gain attention.

In 2019, over 19 different countries are looking at digital fiat currency as an efficient alternative to physical money, to be used as a legal tender. Further improvement as a result of their research and trials is expected to disrupt the financial sector as a whole, especially if it becomes a legal tender in a particular country.

Top challenges in the digital fiat currency industry

As digital fiat currency is still in the process of improving and has yet to be fully implemented, debates and questions on its integrity constantly arise. Issues on regulation, standardization, and its long-term effects to physical, legal tenders continue. Digital fiat is very political as it will disintermediate many established financial industries within the banking ecosystem. They have strong incentives to keep friction in the banking system as it affords them opportunities to make money.

Imposing regulation on digital currencies is a hot political topic because issuing currency grants banks and governments economic control. If anyone could manipulate the supply of money, they could wreak havoc on an economy. Currently, there are 162 central banks globally. Each bank can issue money to their jurisdiction. But, each bank needs to clear and settle balances with other central banks. Utilizing a cryptocurrency, they could move money faster and cheaper between banks. Serious questions arise in the realm of "censorship" and other features that may not be available, depending on the nature of the digital fiat currency.

There are currently several blockchains, distributed ledgers, and centralized options that give banks a wide range of tools and controls to experiment with tokens, cryptocurrency, and other types of digital fiat currency. It will take time to gain agreement on what to use and then create standards around the technology. For this reason, it will be some time before digital fiat currency is available across all countries and it will prove to be a major challenge. But there is hope, Norway's City Coin and Austria's Vienna Token are exciting examples of what is possible. As of present, the United Arab Emirates, Canada, Italy, and South Africa are all exploring cryptocurrency as a digital fiat.

Long-term effects to physical tenders

The business of making money makes money in itself. Central banks need enough capital to work with printing companies in developing the machines they need, and making sure that printed money of an appropriate quality is available to the public. Shifting to digital currency will help lessen the printing costs that the central banks spend per year in physical tender development. However, this may potentially put an end to the tender printing industry, as the demand for physical printing will decrease.

8.2 Disrupters in banking and currency

There are many startups that are looking to adopt blockchain technology and use it to create new efficiencies in banking. They may have disruptive effects on the financial ecosystem, ranging from retail accounts to the very creation of money. In this section we will take a look at a few interesting blockchain banking companies and digital fiat software currencies.

eCurrency

eCurrency is a software and hardware company that offers several centralized services that enable banks to securely issue their own digital fiat currency. The company was started by David Wen. The eCurrency Monarch™ system creates a digital legal tender instrument that enables instant settlement across interoperating parties. The system, like blockchain systems, allows for real-time e-money transparency to the regulators. They have created dashboards and reports that give regulators and issuers the tools and privacy guards that are required by law.

Blockstream - Liquid

Liquid is an inter-exchange settlement network that can be used by central banks. It is used to link together cryptocurrency exchanges and institutions around the world. Liquid is purported to enable faster Bitcoin transactions and the issuance of digital assets such as digital fiat currency.

Ripio

Ripio Credit Network (RCN) is a blockchain-based global credit network, functioning to connect FinTech companies, financial institutions and creditors, to create a transparent and borderless debt market. It uses blockchain technology to help create better lending solutions. Retail creditors are provided with direct access to funding without the need for any third party network, reducing costs on operations and financing.

There are two primary services that Ripio offers, depending on the users of the application. Finance companies can offer loans to their customers from anywhere. They can also gain insights into the global debt markets. Retail users can access liquidity during crypto bear markets. This is an important service for major cryptocurrency holders because during bear market conditions the markets can be extremely thin. It becomes difficult to sell cryptocurrency and doing so can further drive the market down.

Woorton

Woorton is a relatively new cryptocurrency-based company, providing liquidity for members of the general public who are involved in the buying and selling of cryptocurrencies. This French-based startup company practically focuses on crypto-fiat trading and bases its operations on several order-books to ensure fair pricing. Woorton provides access to the cryptocurrency market by dealing with multiple partners and offering better trading prices compared to most trading platforms available.

Woorton offers several services. These include research and analysis, where it provides its customers with insights into the latest marketing trends that will help guide them in handling their accounts. Woorton also presents itself as an efficient liquidity provider, as it offers the best available prices when it comes to cryptocurrency trading. Finally, it offers Market Making as a service, where it provides in-house algorithmic trading that customers may use in liquefying their assets on exchanges.

BABB

BABB is a London-based startup bank. It allows customers to open a digital bank account and gain access to several digital financial-related services. In 2019, it had not yet received accreditation to be formally considered as a bank.

BABB's operations are reportedly built on blockchain and they offer a decentralized platform to customers through its mobile app. It also offers a credit card called the "Black Card", with which customers will be able to spend their fiat currencies as they purchase online or anywhere. It is considered as the first decentralized payment card and is connected to the customer's BABB bank account.

8.3 Blockchain and insurance

Insurance is a contractual arrangement, usually referred to as a policy, that an entity or an individual engages into as a means of financial protection. It allows them to be reimbursed by an insurance company and thus mitigate losses in case something unforeseen happens. This could relate to whatever you decide to insure, be it your life, a house, a company, or your health.

The global insurance market was valued at US$4.8 trillion in 2017 and has increased from 2011 to 2017 at a CAGR (Compound Annual Growth Rate) of 1%. This slow growth is mainly attributed to the constant insured losses, mostly due to force majeure, meaning unforeseeable circumstances that impact you. In fact, in 2017, the USA's insurance industry lost over US$135 billion due to hurricanes, California wildfires, and Mexican earthquakes that prompted reimbursements by insurers.

There are a lot of different kinds of insurances out there. Here is a quick run through the two main categories and their key differences.

Life insurance refers to insurance that provides reimbursement and monetary compensation if there is a risk to life. In the event of the death of the customer or insurer, its beneficiaries will receive a certain amount of cash, either through a lump sum or through periodical installments.

General insurance, on the other hand, refers to any type of insurance that is not categorized as life insurance. This classification is divided into three types: fire insurance in which the contract covers the insurer's reimbursement in case of loss of property and goods due to fire; marine insurance in which the coverage is for anything related to marine misadventure; and miscellaneous insurance which covers practically everything else that the above mentioned insurances do not cover.

History of insurance

The beginning of insurance industry dates back to the time of the Babylonians during 4000 – 3000 BCE. Some of the first types of insurance offered were called "bottomry". These helped to protect merchants while they shipped their goods. Another early type of insurance was for funeral costs. In ancient Rome, individuals would pay their monthly dues and this was an early type of life insurance.

In the 1600s, the idea of imposing insurances in case of fire and plague was conceptualized in the UK after the Great Fire of London destroyed over 14,000 buildings.

In the mid-1700s, the first American insurance company was founded by Benjamin Franklin, which was the first to offer life insurance. This went on for at least a century, closely followed by the foundation of more insurance companies in the United States, but most of them failed due to poor investment and management. This, however, eventually stabilized by the early 1900s, and the industry has enjoyed steady growth since then.

Insurance of the present

Insurance at present is practically everywhere. It is now possible to insure all manner of things ranging from life and health right down to material things such as mobile phones and gadgets. This is because most of these material items are purchased at a specific value, and are often prone to damage. Insurance gives peace of mind in protecting against the cost of such damage.

Insurance of the future

Insurance companies like most industries need to find ways to sell new products at lower costs. DLT and other types of blockchain software may be able to help them to record contracts better and share them with relevant third parties. Other interesting experiments include instant insurance sold from vending machines or an app on your phone. For example, you could purchase insurance for travel or accommodation based on your geolocation, and claims could be processed automatically if something went wrong.

Insurance companies are exploring new products that pay out in advance of natural disasters. For example, you could receive a payment before a storm hits that allows you to better prepare for the event. Each of these new types of products needs integrated systems that can read data from connected devices like your car, a camera, or a data feed from a weather source. DLT and blockchain provide possible solutions as they allow multiple parties to collaborate and share information.

Top challenges in the insurance industry

There are several challenges that the insurance industry are currently facing. Some of these include slow growth, rising customer expectations, and more burdensome regulations. Natural disasters, storms, and accidents have spiked in recent years, further increasing costs. Additional challenges include contextually appropriating risk for novel environments (i.e.

what are appropriate exclusions in a policy). The precepts of custody and their definitions also impact the ability to issue policies.

Increased attention to the industrial process as a whole is the only measure being taken by players in the industry, such as working on enhancing customer satisfaction and encouraging consumer retention. Although it is not clear on how to further improve the industry's situation in the longer term, players in the industry are currently looking at not only further expansion of services on offer, which would help increase their portfolio, but also the number of consumers as a whole.

Blockchain technology is now being explored as a means of lowering overhead costs and allowing insurance companies to squeeze more value out of the contacts that they have already. In particular, attention is focused upon how to establish a credible and easily provable chronological order of events, the authenticity of goods within supply chains, accurate and automated accounting of items within warehouses, and automated and authenticated micro insurance for things like travel and peer-to-peer economy innovations.

Blockchain startup companies in the insurance industry

Several startup companies entered the insurance market to disrupt the industry with the help of blockchain technology. Blockchain's unique approach to handling transactions and operations as a whole provides exceptional value to startups, allowing a faster, more secure, efficient, and transparent way of tracking transactions and documentation.

Black

Black Insurance is a startup company that operates using blockchain technology. It focuses on providing insurance policies through crowdfunding, in which transactions may be carried out using cryptocurrencies. The integration of blockchain technology with the crowdfunding approach to gaining investment capitals for insurance portfolios allows a secure way of distributing securities and reimbursements.

Right now, Black Insurance is still in the process of improving the platform on which customers can work on their policies. Its approach will see Black operate as the platform on which the broker will be able to create a customized insurance contract that is tailored to the customer's needs. The crowd will be able to provide crowdfunds, by paying through tokens, which in turn will be distributed to policyholders as capital.

BlockRe

BlockRe is an insurance startup that mitigates client exposure to crypto asset-related risks, such as private key theft and kidnapping. They also provide specialized underwriting and claims adjusting services to brokers, wholesalers, and carriers who are in the crypto asset and blockchain markets.

B3i

B3i is a startup company aiming to create a better and improved insurance industry by developing protocols and standards to remove friction in risk transfers. It was established in 2017 and is now being shared by customers, companies, and community members all over the world. It aims to optimize the market-wide process of insurance transactions that will help generate significant savings and reduce processing time.

B3i works with a platform through distributed ledger technology. Using this platform effectively eliminates data duplication and, along the way, provides a safe and transparent transaction process. It offers smart contracts, which ensures security and immutability among all of the transactions and documents.

B3i's application, known as the B3i Cat XoL, aims to enable customers to gain access to overpayments and transactions with transparency, certainty, and efficiency. This application will be available for customer use by Q4 2019.

ChainThat

ChainThat is a startup company focusing on the FinTech industry, offering insurance solutions to enable positive changes in the industry. It combines both insurance and technology and approaches it with efficiency to ensure that ChainThat's solution delivers breakthrough efficiency.

ChainThat offers various solutions through its online platform. It provides information through Bermuda Risk Exchange, which presents itself as the world's first technology-driven reinsurance risk and capital exchange. It offers placing that allows brokers and insurers to create, negotiate, and manage placement terms. It also offers accounting, settlement, and claims agreement through a DLT platform, and facility schemes using blockchain technology. It provides contract management, through which parties are allowed to create, negotiate, and manage digital contracts.

8.4 Intellectual property rights and providence

Intellectual property rights, often shortened to IP, is the right that a person or a company has to exclusively control their own plans, ideas, or any intangible assets. IP makes it illegal for others to duplicate your efforts for commercial purposes. Your competitors may not use your idea, but you only have the right to exclusivity for a specific period.

The four types of intellectual property are:
- Trade secrets;
- Trademarks;
- Copyright;
- Patents.

There are two areas that are generally covered by intellectual property rights; the copyright and all rights related therein, and the industrial property rights. Copyright refers to the rights of the authors over literary and artistic works and usually covers at least 70 years after the author's death. The purpose of copyright is to encourage and reward creative work and at the same time, protect the author's craft.

Industrial property rights, on the other hand, have two main areas; one is about the protection of the signs, trademarks, and geographical indications of a business which are used to stimulate and ensure fair competition to protect consumers. The second type is to protect the company's innovation, design, and creation of technology. This is to protect the results of investment brought about by the industry's technology.

History of intellectual property rights

The earliest recorded document on intellectual property law was found from around 500 BCE during the Greek's civilization. Sybaris, a Greek state, allowed a citizen to obtain at least one year's worth of patent for any new refinement in luxury. This effectively protected inventors, artists, and merchants to promote and exchange their ideas exclusively over the given period without any threats of competition.

In 1623, the English Parliament drafted the "Statute of Monopolies" in which the true and first inventor is granted 14 years of exclusive control over any of the inventions that they have created. By 1710, the Statute of Anne was drafted in support of the Statute of Monopolies, which aims to provide another 14 years of renewal after the first 14 year protection period passed.

In 1883, the Paris Convention was held and formed an agreement to expand the protection of the inventors and authors from having their innovations being used in other countries. 1886's Berne Convention expanded the statute to include songs, writings, sculptures, drawings, operas, and paintings. More intangible properties were further included as the agreement was expanded in the Madrid Agreement in 1891.

By the 18th century, it was acknowledged that there was a need for industrial inventions to be protected, which gave birth to patent laws. By then, the decision to provide patents was solely left under the jurisdiction of the officials and judges.

Intellectual property at present

By 1967, a specialized agency was formed by the United Nations to represent and protect the commercial interests of holders, copyrights, trade secrets, trademarks, and patents, called the World Intellectual Property Organization (WIPO). The need for these laws was further strengthened by the advent of the digital era of production, reproduction, and distribution. In 2010, Keith Aoki defined the four areas that form the rubric of the intellectual property to be copyright, patent, trademarks, and trade secrets.

Intellectual property of the future

Blockchain and the internet will play a significant role in intellectual property in the future. The digital era provides broader coverage for intellectual property, including all digital media pieces. Further, blockchain helps provide firm security and protection on all.

Top challenges in the intellectual property rights industry

Intellectual property rights grow continuously over the years. But as the coverage expands, so the industry is faced with several challenges.

Digital reproduction

The problem with the digital era is that everything can now be transferred to digital media, meaning it is straightforward to reproduce almost any kind of music, art, literary piece, or practically any work. The problem with this is that due to the effortless access to these works, thanks to the digitization, the uniqueness of the works tends to lessen as more and more people gain easier access to the said piece. These people, in turn, will have the ability to distribute it to others or even make a perfect copy from their end.

This is a problem that shows up along with the advancement of technology. At present, discussions are taking place on how to properly solve the problem of fraudulent cyber acts. However, there has yet to be an effective global solution to the ever-increasing volumes of cybercrime.

Coverage expansion of rights

As shown by history, intellectual property rights started by only providing exclusive rights to merchants to sell their works for some agreed time without threat of competition. This rapidly changed as new technologies were introduced and shifted to a different era that helped to improve mankind as a whole. These shifts introduced the need to expand the rights from just exclusive selling to other situations where an author or owner had developed new ideas on their own and wished to protect these.

Apart from arts, literary pieces, and industrial rights, other industries need patents such as pharmaceutical compounds, agricultural processes, software, and even methods of medical treatment. These patents are important to ensure that the people who originally conceptualized the ideas will enjoy the full benefits of using their crafts as their own for some time.

It is not surprising that in the next 10 to 20 years, more items will be covered by intellectual property rights through the use of copyrights and patents, especially as discoveries under several different fields are emerging.

Digital IP of the future

IP is grounded in a concept of fairness, "who did what when" and the first person that did something should have the right to the commercial benefit for those efforts. Blockchain technology has at its very core a system of record that allows anyone to begin recording events and information that is time stamped and located into an unalterable state. This functionality can easily be harnessed to record all kinds of information, including the creation of IP.

Blockchain technology can be used as a means of establishing hierarchical authority and enabling payment for utility. In an ever more digital world, this is an exciting way to enable faster and more direct payment for things like music and blueprints for 3D printers.

We'll now take a look at examples of blockchain projects that are rethinking IP and using blockchain technology to improve the system.

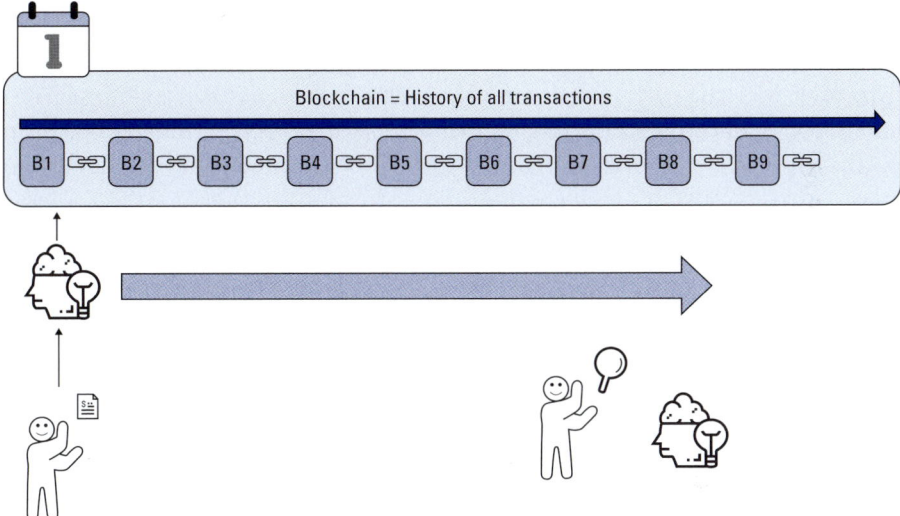

Figure 33   Intellectual property rights and blockchain - you can establish that something existed at a given point in time and third parties can verify that information.

IPwe
IPwe is a blockchain technology company offering a platform as the world's patent ecosystem. Using artificial intelligence, IPwe offers data mining and predictive analysis to create new and innovative ways to interact and transact with patents. IPwe aims to provide a cheaper and faster way to collect and process patent transactions and help fund innovative and secure processes in patent sales. Using blockchain and AI, IPwe intends to make patent processing safer, cheaper, and faster.

IPwe creates a database to record and capture several patent transactions, enabling people to easily see whatever type of patent is needed, its owner, and the coverage of the said patent. It provides details about the said patent, with the worth and validity of the patent. The analytic platform is available to its users free of charge.

LOCI
LOCI is an online directory of patents. It offers a platform that allows users to search, analyze, and file their patents within LOCI's user interface. To change and simplify patent

search, it offers a unique visualization and database gathering with the help of blockchain technology to provide a faster and easier process of patent search.

Through its web platform, LOCI offers visual search for its users through its IP landscape. It is equipped with enhanced filtering and an easy-to-navigate interface to help customers easily find their patents, and improve their ideas. It offers a market and industry overview to help identify how unique your approach will be and how beneficial it is likely to be to your target market.

Vaultitude

Vaultitude is a company that focuses on the legal, patent, and copyright industry, offering optimal legal protection of company data and intellectual property. Using blockchain technology, it provides a safe environment for information sharing, transfer, and management of inventions, data, and corporate documents that need legal protection from non-competition issues. It offers a safer approach to signing legal contracts through blockchain and smart contracts.

Using blockchain technology, Vaultitude intends to provide not only security but also transparency of data to ensure that inventors, authors, and innovators will be able to better protect their intellectual property rights in legal proceedings. Through its database, users can search and obtain the necessary information about any patents, and create digital fingerprints for their files.

8.5 Summary

Blockchain software is impacting on many industries along with functions that governments fulfill. Any place where two or more parties need to cooperate, and there is an opportunity for one party to gain an advantage over another, the right software may be used to improve the process and reduce friction. The blockchain and DLT systems being developed and tested now, will lead to reductions in cost and the elimination of many well-paying and once very secure jobs.

The banking industry has a lot of opportunities for consolidation as they are in the trust business. Individuals and corporations trust banks to hold and send their funds and help remedy issues like bounced checks and credit card fraud. Blockchain and DLT systems can streamline and improve the manual practices banks use every day, particularly when it comes to handling currency. Digital fiat currency may reduce counterfeiting, money laundering, and tax evasion, saving governments and banks untold millions, since it can help to reduce a user's anonymity (and, as a consequence, also his privacy).

The transparency of records within DLT and blockchain systems will need to be balanced with people's right to privacy and anonymity. A future where your car or other IoT devices act as a witness for you in insurance claims is exciting. But on the other hand, having every interaction you make permanently recorded, starts to become dystopian.

DLT and blockchain software can create a better future that is fair and more global. Intellectual property rights recorded and shared using DLT or within a blockchain present the possibility that talented individuals can establish ownership over their work and financially benefit from it in new ways. Many companies are working on creating transparency in royalty distribution for authors, for example.

This chapter has given you some insight into how DLT and blockchain technology are creating new markets and destroying old business models. Armed with this knowledge, you can now better navigate career choices and prepare for a future with digital fiat, smart contract insurance, and global IP protection.

8.6   Test your knowledge

1. **What is digital fiat currency?**
   A. Digital fiat currencies are an incentive paid to miners who maintain the integrity of a public blockchain network.
   B. Digital fiat currencies are a digital representation of the country's fiat currency, which will be backed by financial reserves of the country such as forex and gold.
   C. Digital fiat currencies are a digital representation of a non-fungible smart contract that allows the ownership to be reassigned.
   D. Digital fiat is used by central banks to incur fees.

2. **What is a cryptocurrency?**
   A. A cryptocurrency is an incentive paid to miners who maintain the integrity of a public blockchain network. It is a self-clear, settling, and authenticating data packet.
   B. A cryptocurrency is a digital representation of the country's fiat currency, which will be backed by financial reserves of the country such as forex and gold.
   C. A cryptocurrency is a smart contract that allows the ownership to be reassigned.
   D. A cryptocurrency is a non-fungible digital asset.

3. **What is a token?**
   A. A token is a smart contract that allows the owner to be reassigned. It is a self-clearing, settling, and authenticating data packet.
   B. A token is an incentive paid to miners who maintain the integrity of a public blockchain network. It is self-clearing, settling, and authenticating data packet.
   C. A token is a digital representation of the country's fiat currency, which will be backed by financial reserves of the country such as forex and gold.
   D. A token is a non-fungible smart contract that allows the owner to be reassigned.

4. **What is Bottomry?**
    A. Bottomry is how insurance companies rank contracts.
    B. Bottomry is a type of insurance contract offered to merchants to help protect their investments while it is being shipped.
    C. Bottomry is a type of interest paid on contracts offered to merchants to help protect their investments while it is being shipped.
    D. Bottomry is a type of smart contract offered to merchants to help protect their warehouses.

5. **What drives up the cost of insurance?**
    A. Hurricanes
    B. Floods
    C. Earthquake
    D. Force majeure

6. **How is blockchain reducing cost in the insurance industry?**
    A. Blockchain technology is being used to eliminate data duplication and provide safe and transparent transaction processing.
    B. Tokens are being used to eliminate data duplication and provide safe and transparent transaction processing.
    C. DLT is being used to duplicate data and provide transaction processing.
    D. Blockchain is used to create transparent transactions.

7. **What is Intellectual Property (IP)?**
    A. Intellectual property gives a company control over someone else's plans, ideas, and over intangible assets.
    B. Intellectual property is the rights that a person or a company has to exclusively control their plans, ideas, or over any intangible assets.
    C. IP is the rights that a person has to exclusively control intangible assets.
    D. Intellectual property is the rights that a person or a company has to exclusively control their plans, ideas, or intangible assets.

8. **Why do we have IP rights?**
    A. IP rights reward corporations.
    B. Human rights encourage freedom and creative work.
    C. Property rights encourage and reward ownership.
    D. IP rights encourage and reward creative work.

9. **What are the four types of IP rights?**
    A. Intellectual secrets, bookmarks, copyrights, patents.
    B. Trade secrets, logos, copyrights, patents.
    C. Trade secrets, trademarks, copyrights, patents.
    D. Trade secrets, emblems, copyrights, licenses.

10. **How is blockchain technology being employed in IP rights?**
    A. Blockchain technology allows a user to record an event, such as the creation of IP and establish "who did what when".
    B. A user records IP in a smart contract and establishes ownership globally.
    C. IP allows a user to record the creation of software and establish who did what when.
    D. Blockchain technology allows a user to send a transaction and establish ownership.

9 Blockchain and people

Blockchain innovation has started to impact government infrastructure, citizenship, voting, and health. Smaller countries with more cohesive power have already taken dramatic steps to decentralize their infrastructure and systems.

In this chapter, you will be led through some of the more promising uses of blockchain innovation that you might not have suspected are occurring in government infrastructure, citizenship, voting, and health globally.

9.1 Lean governments

Many smaller countries are capitalizing on the opportunities that trustless transactions and data with providence can provide. In these countries forward-thinking public servants see blockchain technology as an opportunity to streamline their economically expensive bureaucracies. These smaller nations are competing to remain relevant and attractive to both citizens and companies within a global economy where the individual can move and relocate their lives more efficiently than ever before. Such countries are shifting what was once a liability into a strength, for example by having small and nimble legislation to compete to be a jurisdiction of choice. Termed "competitive governance", governments are redefining the traditional ideas of citizenship, anticorruption, and voting. In a world that is moving from hard borders to very porous ones, individuals now have the power to choose where they live and what country they call home, and these jurisdictions are poised to compete effectively for human capital.

Under blockchain and distributed ledger models, citizenship is no longer tied to a physical location. Governments can exist without borders or a physical location. Old ideas of citizenship being tied to a location are evaporating. Many small countries are dealing with the threat of being swallowed by larger and more powerful nations. Distributed networks and digital fiat currency can help them protect their citizens. Blockchain technology and other distributed ledger innovations are being embraced in these areas because they reduce the cost of government by creating more efficient systems that citizens can access quickly anywhere in the world, even if the physical jurisdiction is overrun.

Singapore, Estonia, China, the United Arab Emirates, and Malta are all on the frontier of new government infrastructure. The Smart Nation project in Singapore is creating efficiency in currency and connected IoT devices, and has shifted the way in which the government approaches the delivery of services to its citizens. They view civil service as a "customer's" interaction.

Figure 34   Voting – every vote would be automatically counted and verified.

9.2 Estonia's e-Residency

Estonia is a modest country in the European Union, with only 1.3 million inhabitants. It has restricted natural resources, money, and human capital to meet all the needs of its citizens. Their membership is a boon, but the Estonian government saw the need to use technology to create as much transparency and anticorruption as possible. Their efforts have now exceeded the capabilities of many larger nations. Specifically, Estonia launched digital ID cards for online services and has offered citizenship as a service by being the first country to offer e-Residency. They create a digital identity, available to anyone in the world interested in operating a business online and through the European Union. This program allows Estonia to export the benefits of living in a first world nation as an online service. Getting an Estonia e-Residency only takes a few minutes, and the background checks cost around US$100.

Having the e-Residency card does not make you a citizen of Estonia, but it does give you many of the benefits of banking in the EU. Estonia invested heavily in new technology after it exited the Soviet Union. They developed the "single-window principle" that gives each person in Estonia one point of access for all their government and banking needs. The single-window allows access to all tax, legal, and customs services options for citizens via a single secure log-in online. It is easy and paper free. Everything the government provides, except marriage and real estate purchases, can be done entirely online.

The Estonians have embraced blockchain technologies. The next significant development will be a distributed, ledger cloud. Ericsson, Apcera, and Guardtime are jointly developing and operating the Estonian blockchain hybrid platform. It will enhance the scalability, resilience, and data security of tax reporting and online health care advice.

Nasdaq is developing blockchain services in Estonia as well. It's building a market for private companies that keeps track of securities like bonds, equities, and real estate investment trusts (REITs). This new system will allow companies to raise capital and investors to settle transaction immediately. It's also improving the proxy voting process for enterprises.

9.3 Better authentication and notarization in China

China has an affectionate disdain for cryptocurrency, but they love blockchain. Chinese citizens took to ICO investing as it offered them potentially lucrative returns and let them avoid taxation and monetary limits. The Chinese government has tightened regulation around the use of cryptocurrencies, while simultaneously embracing blockchain technology.

An exciting example of its early use was by Ancun Zhengxin. The company performs electronic data notarization services in China. It has partnered with hundreds of traditional notarial offices across 28 provinces and utilizes electronic data storage and blockchain notarization solutions.

Ancun publishes records in a publicly searchable blockchain. These documents allow users to go back and check the authenticity and age of notarization, proving provenance and generating greater trust. Many startups are working on similar concepts in the United States. For example, Tierion.com and Factom let you hash and time-stamp data. Both these solutions anchor the data in Bitcoin blockchain via their own smaller blockchain networks.

9.4 The trust layer for the internet

The internet has been built in layers, each making it more vibrant and accessible for the average person. The blockchain is the next layer of the internet. It is revolutionary since blockchain technologies allow for individuals, governments, and business to all work together in a fair and open manner without first establishing trust, ownership, and authority. Blockchain is the trust layer. However, just as HTTPS and other important innovations are also revolutionary, blockchains themselves may fade quietly out of the public's consciousness as the networks are simply backends to seamlessly interface with technology.

9.5 Spam-free email

You are likely to hate spam and spend countless hours cleaning your inbox and blocking unwanted emails. Often even missing the things you want to attend to. You may worry about the security of your current email systems. At the end of 2016 Yahoo suffered one of the world's largest hacks, with one billion user accounts compromised and all the user data exposed.

Creating a secure email service that is still user friendly is a compelling use case for blockchain technology. A legendary and often very controversial and colorful character in online security has taken on the challenge. Dr. John McAfee, the antivirus software pioneer and social media influencer has created a new platform for email based on blockchain technology.

SwiftMail (www.swiftcoin.club) was originally named John McAfee SwiftMail, but has since removed McAfee as an adviser. They have created a blockchain-based email inside a cryptocurrency wallet.

There are many new initiatives with better user interfaces that are building email and messaging apps. Pillar is a beautiful example, and you should give it a try. You can find it at https://pillarproject.io/wallet. These apps aren't that different from the email and messaging apps you already use, but they do add in payment and authorization features that normal email has yet to embrace.

They can provide these extra benefits because they use blockchain or other distributed layer technologies. For example, SwiftMail's blockchain confirms that your mail is genuine and that the emails you sent were received by the intended parties, removing the need to trust a third party, like Yahoo!, with your data. There is a small inherent cost to send an email that desensitizes spammers. Pillar has a unique built-in blockchain explorer that alerts both parties that funds are on their way. This is an improvement over waiting on a transaction to be confirmed in a block.

These apps allow you to take a strong stance on your privacy and prevent service providers from exploiting your data.

9.6 Blockchain oracles for IoT

Blockchain technology doesn't solve the problem that information must come from somewhere. It's essential that the data can be relied on. It's the human element that can't yet be removed from the equation when you want to act on a contract within a blockchain system.

There is no central authority to police or enforce honesty in a blockchain system. Predicting the future trustworthiness of the authors of information is impossible. The logical conclusion is that each transaction must cost less than the cost to rebuild a reputation. The reputations of trusted authors are built over time, and the longer an author is honest and correct, the more valuable the author's reputation becomes. This concept is similar to the value of a name brand.

9.7 IP and trusted authorship

Smart contracts and chain codes have created a new opportunity for knowledgeable individuals and corporations to monetize their information. These types of systems need trusted sources of information to execute. These trusted sources could be rating agencies, weather outlets, or just about anything else.

You could connect IoT devices to blockchain infrastructure and have them create their voices and identities on a blockchain network. They need to build trust over time and can still be fabricated at any given point. It is important to understand that past honesty doesn't prevent future dishonesty or the corruption of a source of information.

Not all smart contracts or chain codes are self-contained or execute against authoritative sources. The more practical and applicable business use case require information to be derived from sources outside the known universe of any given blockchain network. Several startups are attacking this problem from different angles.

Po.et is a startup that is building a decentralized protocol for content ownership, discovery, and monetization, intended for artists and creatives. This system is designed to record and time-stamp metadata and ownership information about creative assets, such as writing and music.

Factom has created Acolyte and other API services that allow users to build a reputation over time for the information they provide to the network. Smart contract builders can subscribe and compensate oracles that are built. They can rate them for their trustworthiness.

From a dramatically different angle, Augur, another blockchain startup, has pioneered the idea of prediction markets. Augur is a platform that rewards users for predicting future real-world events such as an election or corporate buyouts. The bets are made by trading virtual shares on the outcome of events. Users make money by buying shares in the correct results. The cost of the shares fluctuates based on how the community feels about the likelihood of the event actually happening. Augur is similar to a betting website in that anyone can make a prediction and anyone can create a prediction market for any given event. This would allow you as a business owner, for example, to take a poll on what event or outcome people think is most likely to occur. It may uncover inside information that authors would like to be able to capitalize on.

9.8 Intellectual property rights

One of the hardest-hit industries that is struggling with intellectual property rights is the music industry. Artists at the top are squeezed out economically by the many intermediaries that rely on their creative work. Less successful artists (with a smaller audience) can't make music a primary source of income because they only see a small fraction of the revenue they generate. Megastars make it on the sheer volume of fans.

The internet has made it easier for artists with different sized fan bases to share their work. At the same time, it has made it even harder for people to make a comfortable living doing what they love. The music industry food chain is a long one, and each intermediary takes a small piece of the pie, which adds to the length of time that it takes for funds to eventually reach the artist. Often, the artist will wait up to 18 months or more to see any money and may only get US$0.000035 per instance of his/her music being streamed. This situation is a best-case scenario in our current market, with no one defrauding the artist.

Blockchain has been proposed as a way to help lighten the heavy financial burden on creatives. Cryptocurrency could be used to reduce transaction fees associated with credit cards and fraud. It would open up new markets in developing countries that don't have regular access to credit cards.

An even more impressive but less straightforward possibility would be migrating the whole music industry ecosystem onto a blockchain system that utilizes smart contracts or chain code to facilitate immediate payment for consumption. It could clarify ownership of licenses and make it easier for consumers to license music for commercial use.

Several projects are working on this issue and looking to promote a healthy, sustainable, and frictionless ecosystem — one that does not displace market players but does allow artists to gain a bit more reward from their hard work.

UjoMusic is beta testing its platform that lets users sell and license music directly. It utilizes the Ethereum network, smart contracts for execution, and Ether (the Ethereum cryptocurrency) for payment. You can download a whole song or just the vocal and instrumental stems for commercial or non-commercial use. The musicians are then paid immediately with Ether.

Peertracks is another blockchain startup that's working on changing the music industry. It's a music streaming website that allows users to download and discover new artists. It does this through its peer-to-peer network called MUSE and the creation of individual artist tokens. These tokens work like other cryptocurrency and fluctuate in value depending on the popularity of the artist.

Blockchain technology doesn't remove the need for music labels and distributors. However, the original companies will need to act swiftly if they don't want to be displaced by new companies that readjust to this more efficient model, just as Netflix disrupted Blockbuster.

9.9 Government

In this section, you will get an introduction to the exciting innovations that are occurring inside governments and cities around the world. You will learn more about the organizations that support them with innovative blockchain projects.

Governments are fighting back against cybercrime and identity theft using blockchain technology and distributed ledger systems. They are using blockchains to underpin smart city initiatives, which will be critical to economic growth. Smart cities, e.g. Hangzhou and Singapore, are taking advantage of modern technology to enhance infrastructure function, and safety, and improve traffic and air quality. The business of becoming a smart city is booming, and almost every larger municipality has embraced the smart city concept and considered using blockchain or distributed ledger technology.

Smart cities of China - Hangzhou

Wanxiang, a Chinese part manufacturer, is utilizing a blockchain protocol to develop data infrastructure for a smart city project in the city of Hangzhou. They are utilizing an off-chain/ on-chain strategy to secure sensitive data from identification cards and smart equipment. They are recording driving behavior and using the data to train autonomous driving systems. The network they are using is PlatON. The PlatON system decouples computation from consensus, unlike Ethereum where smart contracts are computed within the system. This allows them to reduce inherent cost and scale to lots of low-value data sources like IoT devices. The procedure is as follows:

1. Users deploy and release a meta smart contract. The contract has parameters, functions, and economic incentives.
2. Then users call their smart contract and send their transactions.
3. Computing nodes execute the smart contract and generate the proof. These nodes are not inside the blockchain.
4. The computing nodes send the results to other nodes that are in the blockchain. These nodes are "on-chain".
5. The on-chain block producing nodes then verify the results.
6. The verified results are returned to the user via a smart contract.
7. The blockchain then sends economic rewards according to the value of computing contribution from the nodes that verified results.

U.S. Department of Homeland Security

The U.S. Department of Homeland Security is investigating the securing of data feeds that are produced by IoT devices using blockchain technology.

One project is combining blockchain technology with IoT infrastructure used to protect the U.S. Border. This includes IoT devices such as ground sensors and cameras.

By writing the data to a blockchain and having the devices cryptographically sign the data that they send, DHS is eliminating the ability to spoof or modify the information they collect from ground sensors and cameras. This is an important innovation as it helps prevent human trafficking and the movement of illicit goods.

Singapore's Smart Nation project
Singapore was one of the first jurisdictions to see the potential for, and embrace blockchain technology. They have a distinctly positive view and are encouraging and recruiting FinTech companies to experiment. The Monetary Authority of Singapore (MSA) has created a regulatory sandbox that allows them to closely monitor the experiments undertaken by startups that would like to create new financial products and services.

A potentially ground shaking experiment they are conducting at the MAS is Project Ubin. They are creating Central Bank Digital Money using distributed ledger technology (DLT). The project will allow for nearly instant clearing and settlement of payments and securities.

The first phase of the project started in 2016 where they proved the ability to conduct a domestic inter-bank payment using a central bank-issued SGD equivalent token. The banks and corporations involved included Bank of America Merrill Lynch, Credit Suisse, DBS Bank, The Hongkong And Shanghai Banking Corporation Limited, J.P. Morgan, Mitsubishi UFJ Financial Group, OCBC Bank, R3, Singapore Exchange, UOB Bank, and BCS Information Systems as a technology provider to the project.

Project Ubin then expanded in 2017 and developed software prototypes for three different models for decentralized inter-bank payment and settlements. The new software created better liquidity for the banks. They developed a Delivery versus Payment (DvP) that is able to settle tokenized assets across different blockchain platforms. The software prototype allows financial institutions to simultaneously exchange and settle tokenized digital currencies and securities. Project Ubin demonstrated that DvP settlement finality, interledger interoperability, and investor protection could be achieved through utilizing blockchain technology.

Project Ubin was used in 2018 to carry out a cross-border Payment versus Payment (PvP) with the Bank of Canada, Bank of England, and the MAS. It was again successful and demonstrated nearly immediate settlement, reduced cost and increased transparency for all parties.

Singapore satellite cities in India
The Indian government launched a smart cities initiative in 2015 with Enterprise Singapore, with the intention of building 99 new smart cities. The initiative has US$40 billion to fund all its projects. The projects are expected to attract another US$90 billion in foreign investment.

India's population is becoming more urbanized and to prevent these cities from becoming overcrowded and unlivable, they are developing smart cities. The government is introducing more central planning and better-connected infrastructure. The infrastructure upgrades will include low-energy housing, smart grids, transportation, integrated IT systems, e-governance, and better water harvesting.

Singapore will help to develop a new capital in the southeast of India called Amaravati. The project has been under development for three years and requires another US$15 billion dollars. These projects could dramatically improve the lives of millions of people but are extremely expensive to implement and can't be completed overnight.

Indian authorities have engaged a team of Singaporeans to develop a satellite town in Himachal Pradesh. It will cover 20 hectares and is hoped to relieve the congestion in Shimla, a city that has had a massive population rise in the past few decades. The project includes educational, residential, and commercial development.

China's Whole Country strategy

Blockchain technology has had a love-hate relationship in China. In 2017 blockchain mining and ICOs were expelled from the country and professionals in the space were arrested. At the same time, China's government has invested heavily in blockchain development. They are leading in innovation and cracking down on blockchain systems they can't control. The Cyberspace Administration of China (CAC) released a list of nearly 200 registered blockchain service providers that had been approved. They created regulations for the management of these blockchain service providers.

China's approach is not to have a decentralized and autonomous system but rather to disintermediate western rule-of-law-based systems. China is implementing supply-chain management, tax collection, and food safety using blockchain technology. China's Development Bank signed a memorandum of understanding for blockchain research collaboration with Brazil, Russia, India, and South Africa. And they are potentially looking to utilize this technology in their "One Belt - One Road" global strategy for economic growth and influence.

9.10 Financial capitals of the world

Blockchain technology has given governments a new competitive tool. And the race for relevance has heated up. The last decade has seen populations shifting to jurisdictions that are more livable and safer. People globally are now more mobile and financially fluid. Many countries understand the impact that blockchain technology can have on financial systems. Malta, Singapore, Dubai, and London all welcome FinTech innovation and are competing to be the financial center of the world. Each has put together formal initiatives and programs to attract and retain talent and make sure that innovation happens within their countries. Nearly 2,000 new blockchain startups formed overnight in 2016 during the ICO crazy. Those not washed out in fraud and financial crimes are working on beta and pre-launch initiatives that are just now being used to overhaul centralized systems.

London

The United Kingdom embraced blockchain technology early. In 2016, the central government of the UK put out a report called "Distributed Ledger Technology: Beyond Block Chain" which affirmed that distributed ledger technology could be used to reduce corruption, errors, and fraud. The report claimed that DLT would change the relationship of citizens with their government by bringing about more transparency and trustworthiness. Many blockchain startups moved operations to London in 2014 because it was the safest place to build. This was significant at that time because many cryptocurrency entrepreneurs were imprisoned in 2014 and 2015 in the U.S.

Blockchain technology has even been approved for use across government applications in the UK. First implementations outside of financial technology will be with Whitehall departments that are non-ministerial departments. This includes Land Registry, Forestry Commission, and Food Standards, local authorities, and delegated governments.

Exciting projects across the UK

There are a number of interesting blockchain projects in the UK, including:
- Blockchain-based welfare distribution: the Department of Work and Pensions has partnered with Barclays, RWE, GovCoin, and the University of London.
- Government DLT: Credits, a blockchain platform provider, and the UK government are collaborating on DLT stands for distributed ledger technology.
- Blockchain-based international payments: Santander Bank has started a trial of blockchain-based international payments. The staff pilot program involves using Apple Pay.
- Trading gold: the Royal Mint is working with CME Group to use blockchain technology to build a gold market.

9.11 Dubai's 2020 goal

The Crown prince of UAE, Sheikh Hamdan, set out an ambitious plan in 2017 to make Dubai the world's first blockchain government by 2020. The Smart Dubai initiative is a public-private partnership to transform Dubai into a smart city. The effort is working to create a seamless experience for its citizens as they interact with government services. Blockchain technology will be essential in allowing them to move all government documents and systems by 2020. The plan is to issue its last paper transaction in 2021 and save the country approximately US$1.5 billion in document processing.

The UAE's Ministry of Cabinet Affairs and Future created a detailed plan to allow citizens to update and verify their identity credentials through the blockchain. Once complete, UEA citizens will be able to log in with their credentials and access both government and regulated private companies like insurance companies and banks. The technology developed by the initiative is planned to be shared with other countries to enable things like easier and faster border crossings. Travelers may use a digital wallet with identification features instead of a passport. Overall the UEA government estimates their blockchain initiative will save 25.1 million hours in productivity for the country.

UEA's Global Blockchain Council (GBC) has many public-private collaborations:
1. Healthcare: Dubai's largest telecom operator, Du, is working with an EU company, Guardtime to digitize healthcare records using blockchain technology.
2. Diamond trade: the Dubai Multi Commodities Center will be securing Kimberly certificates used by the UN to restrict the trade of conflict diamonds.
3. Land titles: title transfers will be digitized and secured on a blockchain.
4. Business registration: as part of their paperless initiative, businesses will be able to register in the UAE, and blockchain will be fully used to secure those records.
5. Tourism: Dubai Points is a token travel reward program for tourists.
6. Shipping: under the SMART Borders initiative, they are exploring smart contracts to improve shipping by allowing near-instant settlement and allowing them to enhance other aspects of trade, travel, and transport.

Over the last two years, UAE has worked hard and dedicated resources to the Smart Dubai initiative. With a centralized power structure, they have been able to move towards decentralization quickly.

9.12 BitLicense of New York City

The New York Department of Financial Services (NYDFS) has created a special application process for companies that are developing blockchain technology called a Bitlicense. It gives companies a regulatory framework for digital currency. The license costs US$5,000 and is 500 pages long. It requires the fingerprints of each of the company's leaders and an extensive background check. There is an additional US$100,000 in expenses associated with the application. This estimate includes time allocation, legal, and compliance fees. The US's BitLicense for NYC is in stark contrast to the efforts made by other financial centers such as London, Singapore, and Dubai that have recruited and welcomed blockchain technology.

The BitLicenses have been challenging to obtain, and in the last four years, only 18 have been granted. On a positive note, the NYDFS no longer requires software companies to gain approval for things like software patches.

The first company to receive a Bitlicense was Circle, the bitcoin wallet providers. They have since gone on to issue a stable token called the USDC. It allows you to transfer dollars anywhere in the world in minutes instead of days. The USDC uses an Ethereum smart contract standard (ERC-20) that will enable it to work with wallets and exchanges globally. Circle holds a reserve equivalent to the circulation of USDC in regulated financial institutions. USDC is a powerful tool for crypto traders who leverage the stability of US dollars.

The FinTech company Ripple received the second Bitlicense. They operate a hybrid blockchain that provides a central bank role for banks allowing them to settle transactions quickly. The license was essential for Ripple because many of their banking customers are headquartered or operate in NYC.

Overall the U.S. has been slow and reluctant to adopt blockchain for financial technology. California bill AB 1326 would have been similar to the Bitlicense but failed after the Electronic Frontier Foundation (EFF) was able to oppose it. The EFF is a group based in San Francisco that defends customer rights and new technology.

9.13 Malta, the blockchain island of the EU

The European Union's member country Malta has taken drastic and direct steps to embrace blockchain technology. Moving much quicker than other larger nations, they saw the potential of blockchain could have for them and took steps to secure themselves as a hub for innovation. Many American and Chinese companies have flocked to Malta to set up businesses. This includes the mega-exchange Binance which has obtained cryptocurrency license that gives it better access to the EU.

There are three key documents that provide protection and legal frameworks for blockchain technology companies, the Virtual Financial Assets Act, the Malta Digital Innovation Authority Act, and the Technology Arrangements and Services Bill.

1. The Virtual Financial Assets Act regulates initial coin offerings (ICOs).
2. The Malta Digital Innovation Authority Act creates regulatory procedures for cryptocurrency and blockchain companies. It established a regulatory body called the Malta Digital Innovation Authority (MDIA).
3. Technology Arrangements and Services Bill allows blockchain companies and cryptocurrency exchanges to register with the Malta government.

Malta's actions have made it one of the hottest new jurisdictions for blockchain.

9.14 German blockchain

The German government has mostly been ambivalent to blockchain technology. They have put out warnings for initial coin offerings (ICO) Ponzi schemes. This is a type of fraud that was very common during 2016-2018 where early investors were lead to believe that the success of a non-existent enterprise would give them a quick profit from money invested by later investors. In the blockchain space, this is called "pump and dump".

An interesting new initiative by the German Federal Ministry of Finance may change German securities laws. They published a report on the treatment and regulation of blockchain-based securities. The document may pave the way for new types of financial products. They propose enacting new blockchain technology regulations for "digital value right". These new rules would make it possible for bonds, which are printed on paper to be issued digitally on a blockchain.

9.15 French blockchain efforts

France is lobbying the EU to adopt a regulatory framework for blockchain technology and cryptocurrencies. The French parliament approved a financial sector law that they hope will attract FinTech companies to set up shop. The new law gives entrepreneurs official recognition and allows the country to tax their profits.

The French government's new bill is considered to be the first adopted by a major nation. This is a big step towards mainstream acceptance because many major jurisdictions have banned cryptocurrency and token offering, or have yet to recognize them officially.

The French government has committed to help support the development of blockchain technology. The finance minister of France has allocated 4.5 billion euros towards this effort. The investments will be granted to companies building blockchain innovations over the next half-decade. France would like to be a global leader in the blockchain ecosystem and compete with Chinese and American technological companies.

9.16 Summary

Blockchain technology is now being experimented with by governments. Many believe that it can be used to dramatically cut the cost of regulation, auditing, and enforcement. This chapter has explored some of the latest innovations from around the world that look to cut cost and improve systems for governments and large corporations. It has also explored government regulation of blockchain technology and how that has changed over time.

This chapter is essential to understand the bigger picture of how blockchain is changing governments, regulations, and global commerce. It is fundamental to helping you gain a deeper understanding of how governments and large corporations are treating blockchain technology.

9.17 Test your knowledge

1. **What is the Estonian e-Residency?**
   A. An Estonian government program to grant citizenship.
   B. An Estonian government program to allow non-EU residents to live in Europe.
   C. An Estonian government program to allow digital citizenship to non-Estonians. The program enables non-EU residents to benefit from the European banking system.
   D. An Estonian government program to build blockchain technology.

2. **Does Estonian e-Residency make you a citizen of Estonia?**
   A. Yes
   B. No

3. **What is the organization that enforces the rules in a blockchain system?**
   A. There is no central authority to police or enforce honesty in a blockchain system.
   B. The U.S. government.
   C. The Hyperledger Foundation.
   D. The bitcoin core development team.

4. **What is the Virtual Financial Assets Act of Malta?**
   A. It regulates securities.
   B. It regulates FinTech startups.
   C. It regulates initial coin offerings (ICOs).
   D. It regulates blockchains.

5. **What is the Malta Digital Innovation Authority Act?**
   A. It creates regulatory procedures for public blockchains.
   B. It creates regulatory procedures for cryptocurrency and blockchain companies. It established a regulatory body called the Malta Digital Innovation Authority (MDIA).
   C. It creates regulatory procedures for ICOs and establishes a regulatory body called the Malta Digital Innovation Authority (MDIA).
   D. It establishes a regulatory body called the Malta Digital Origination Power.

6. **What is the Technology Arrangements and Services Bill of Malta?**
   A. Technology Arrangements and Services Bill allows blockchain companies and cryptocurrency exchanges to register with Malta government.
   B. It allows cryptocurrency to be deposited in bank accounts.
   C. It gave the Malta government the ability to build blockchain-backed voting systems.
   D. The Technology Arrangements and Services Bill allows U.S. citizens to purchase ICO tokens.

10 Blockchain and the inhibitors

The blockchain industry is often exuberant and exciting. The opportunity to create new products and services has attracted the attention of millions of people, perhaps including you. The fast-paced changes in technology and the increased ease of use has allowed more people to get involved and create new businesses. However, not all those businesses have been for the good of the public.

This chapter looks in more detail at the inherent vulnerabilities of public and private blockchains. You will gain a wider understanding of community fractures and how these feuds can affect your business. This chapter also uncovers many of the common types of fraud and scams that you need to be aware of in order to protect yourself and your business.

In addition, you will uncover many of the challenges and hidden dangers that are specific to the blockchain industry. You will learn more about strategies to avoid some of the traps and pit falls. The knowledge you will have after reading this part will give you the tools to navigate the often Wild-West frontier of blockchain technology.

10.1 Blockchain vulnerabilities

Blockchains are often believed to be hack proof and infallible. This is not true at all, and you would be negligent not to fully understand the vulnerabilities that these types of networks inherently have. In this section, you will gain a deep un-understanding of three key vulnerabilities to the software that runs blockchains and distributed ledgers. You will learn different techniques that you can deploy to help mitigate these risks. Specifically, you will understand how smart contracts can be robbed, how public blockchains can be broken, and some of the fallacies associated with private blockchains.

Smart contract vulnerabilities
Smart contracts are one of the most important innovations to come out of blockchain technology. They allow the creator to program in just about anything you can imagine and because the code that makes up the smart contracts live inside a blockchain network, the code gains the same properties as the blockchain it is built within.

One of the critical strengths of smart contracts is also their greatest weakness. The code within them is exceptionally resilient to manipulation once the contract is deployed. The contracts can only be changed if the blockchain they are deployed on is compromised or they have built-in admin powers. Code by nature is flawed and can be executed in unexpected ways. It takes rigorous testing before smart contracts are ready to be used. The standardization of smart contracts, like the ERC20 on Ethereum, has helped alleviate some of the issues that were caused by faulty code. However, you should always have your smart contracts audited if they are used to secure value such as tokens.

One of the most famous flops was a smart contract called the DAO. The DAO was one of the first examples of a distributed autonomous organization. It contained several smart contracts that were intended to allow inventors to vote on new Ethereum projects and fund them. The DAO was hacked in June 2016, and millions of ether were stolen. This hack claimed approximately 15% of all ether in circulation at the time. The DAO was drained when a clever developer discovered a flaw in the code that allowed him to tap off cryptocurrency by executing the contract in an unexpected manner.

The Ethereum foundation faced a tough choice. The only way they could recover the funds lost in the DAO hack was to hard fork the network and send back the balances to investor's accounts. They chose to do this given the early stage of the network. The choice was devastating to the value of the Ethereum cryptocurrency and brought up many questions about legitimacy and permanence.

Not all smart contracts issuers will have the power and influence to hard fork a network if their smart contract is broken. Smart contracts are a new field with few security standards, documentation, and best practices. Even now, smart contract issuers can inadvertently freeze wallets and break contracts themselves. Hundreds of millions of dollars in value has forever been locked inside inaccessible wallet addresses or has been stolen due to mistakes in smart contract creation.

Centralized public networks

Proof of Work (PoW) public blockchains are only as strong as they are decentralized. The number of independent nodes that have a full history of the network and are actively validating transactions directly affects the security of the whole network. Once a network becomes too concentrated, then criminal minors can corrupt the network with impunity. This particular type of vulnerability is called a 51% attack. 51% is the magical number that creates a tipping point for many blockchains. If fewer than that number of nodes are independent, then a network will be rolled back.

One of the reasons PoW blockchains experience this is because mining using this consensus algorithm puts node operators in a cannibalistic arms race. Each new node that enters the network increases the difficulty of winning the block rewards and, in effect, proportionally makes it more expensive. When networks become more costly to mine than the value that can be derived from selling the cryptocurrency, node operators turn off their miners.

Another strategy that many miners utilize is mining pools. These are groups of miners who combine their hashing power and then proportionally share a reward. This allows operators to gain a more predictable return on their investment. The mining pools then have gained a tremendous amount of power and can affect the future of the blockchain.

Until 2019 51% attacks were more theoretical than actual. But the crash in the price of all cryptocurrencies and the banning of mining in some countries created an opportunity for bad actors. A very popular PoW blockchain, Ethereum Classic, was taken over. The bad miner was able to roll back the history transactions and reassign themselves the Ether Classic.

The attacker did this by gaining control of more than 51% of the network's computing power. This type of attack allowed the users to spend the same cryptocurrency more than once, an issue that is known as "double spends". The attacker oddly enough returned half of the funds a few days later. This strange event caused many to believe that this devastating event was done for fun.

Other consensus algorithms are also vulnerable. For example, EOS experienced a network take-over. With its 21 designated nodes, EOS is maybe even more prone to network centralization and manipulation.

Centralized private networks
Centralized networks don't have the same issues as public networks, but that does not mean they are infallible. A contributing factor is that networks such as Hyperledger's Fabric don't have cryptocurrency. With little to steal, hackers are less incentivized to break the network.

Like many public blockchains, private blockchains have limited financial resources. For example, the Hyperledger security team is a handful of volunteers. The team is relatively responsive in that they undertake to get back to you in two days if you experience a problem. But as their own documentation states, it may take them two months to even put out a bug bounty. Bug bounties are rewards offered to the community of open source developers to identify security issues in the network.

Another issue that you will need to keep in mind is that private blockchains are more like trust networks. The members of the network are known, and contracts can be changed. They do offer improvements compared to paper-based business processes, but they don't have the same finality or enforceability as public networks.

Private networks also have different incentive systems from public networks. On Hyperledger, for example, transactions are validated by the parties to the transaction. Without an incentivized disinterested third party, i.e. the "miner", it is conceivable that nodes in a private network may collude to benefit at the expense of another.

10.2 Community fractures and feuds

One of the greatest threats to the blockchain community is the narcissism of small differences. This idea is that communities with adjoining territories and close relationships are more likely to fight. These communities are more likely to ridicule and mock one another and become hypersensitive to esoteric minutiae.

If you have spent any amount of time on social channels for public blockchain networks, like Twitter, Reddit, or Telegram, you will quickly see many of those engaged are radicalized. Bitcoin itself is as much a cult, a political statement, and a cool technology. And as such it has attracted an interesting mix of individuals.

The rifts in the communities go all the way down to the code. And this has divided the community repeatedly, with many hard forks over the years. New versions of Bitcoin pop up, and they fracture mining power. The new blockchains weaken demand and support for the cryptocurrency. Some amount of discourse can be healthy; however, when the price of a currency falls below the cost to generate it, the network loses miners and the overall integrity of the blockchain becomes compromised.

What is described above is actually a best-case scenario. It does not account for blockchain warfare. One community will attack another and not just on Twitter. For example, it is believed that EOS supporters attacked the Ethereum blockchain by spamming the Ethereum network to drive up the price of transactions and to slow down the speed of smart contract execution. Ethereum experienced thousands of "airdrops" from random ICO tokens that had no companies or projects. It is estimated the attackers spent hundreds of thousands of dollars to spam Ethereum and oddly enough the attack ended on the day EOS was launched.

Bitcoin and all its offspring have experienced the effects of blockchain warfare. A particularly odd and harmful practice is for rogue miners, those not incentivized by block rewards, to produce fake blocks that fracture the network. The network fractures because unexpecting miners get tricked into mining fake versions of their blockchain. Some blockchains have begun introducing software updates that create "checkpoints". Miners check back every ten blocks to make sure they are validating the correct chain. If miners see blocks that don't match the last checkpoint version of the blockchain, these blocks are rejected.

10.3 Fraud and scams

I hope that after reading through this book, you are encouraged to dive deeper into blockchain and distributed ledger technology. The global and distributed nature of this technology has allowed for whole new ways of looking at the world and opportunities to build and create new businesses. However, the newness of it does not make the industry immune to some of the oldest social problems. Pioneering a new frontier is inherently both exciting and dangerous.

In this section, you will discover how old crimes are unfolding in new ways across the blockchain industry. You will get a better understanding of token scams and how to avoid common fraud.

Advanced fee schemes

The blockchain industry has seen its share of advanced fee schemes. In this scam, a fraudster convinces you to pay money for something in anticipation of receiving something of greater value at a later time. In the end, you as the victim receive nothing.

During the ICO craze of 2017-2018, it was common for individuals to promote themselves as investors. They would tell victims that they could get early or exclusive access to investment opportunities in different blockchain projects. They often called it a "pre-sale" and promised investors 30%-90% discounts for being early investors. They frequently promised that their investments would be "unlocked" so early investors could take advantage of the market bump once the tokens were trading on a crypto exchange. In this particular type of fraud, these dubious individuals would never deliver the tokens to the victim.

Fraudsters prey on greed and excitement. They rush you into hasty decision-making and try and create artificial scarcity for what they are offering. There are a number of simple ways in which you can protect yourself from this type of fraud. When anyone is promising returns or early access, they are probably trying to scam you. If the individual does not perform KYC or AML on you (making sure you are accredited and documenting your identity) and presents you with a contract, they are more than likely trying to scam you. If they promise early access, or that your investment will be unlocked, again this is almost certainly a scam, or even worse, they are transferring liability to you as an investor. Every country has different rules for investors, but many require you to hold an investment for at least a year, or you as an investor take on the same liability as the issuers. It's best to consult legal counsel regarding all investments.

Identity theft and credit card fraud

In this scam, a fraudster steals your credit card and uses it to fraudulently obtain money, goods or property. Many credit card companies banned the purchase of bitcoins because thieves were using stolen credit card numbers to fund these purchases.

The thief would often use what is known as "dark pools" to launder the bitcoins. Dark pools are where many different transactions are bundled together outside the blockchain. By sending bitcoins to dark pools, it makes it difficult for authorities to trace the transactions on the blockchain.

With so many people's personal details and identities compromised, it is advisable to add extra protection to bank accounts and credit cards. Many companies offer enhanced features that make it more difficult for unauthorized changes to your account and fraudulent charges to occur. Inquire with your cell phone provider and financial institutions to see how they can better protect your identity and property.

Internet and device hacking

Tokens and cryptocurrency are only as secure as your device and internet connection. It became common for hackers to target wealthy individuals who they believed had cryptocurrencies and tokens. These thieves understood that if they could take over cryptocurrency wallets through hacking devices or internet connections, they could steal an individual's property. It was extremely attractive as there was little to no protection for investors who were robbed.

One common threat was "sim card hacks". Fraudsters would call cellular service providers and pretend to be you. The thieves would then change your account settings and take over your phone, receiving all your calls and text messages. They could send out messages from your number requesting funds from your contacts.

If you had taken a picture of your private keys, passwords, or seed recovery phrase, the thieves could use it to get into your accounts and steal your funds. Often, by looking through cloud backups they could obtain pictures you thought you had deleted.

In more extreme cases, they could hack into your wireless network or one of your connected devices. In this scenario, again the thieves could gain access to your personal information and steal your funds. Higher security devices do not have wireless or blue tooth capabilities. It is wise to keep your devices unplugged and powered down when not in use. If you hold your cryptocurrency on a computer, remove all non-essential software, and utilize a VPN.

Market manipulation

All non-stable tokens and cryptocurrencies have experienced "pump and dump" and still do to this day. A pump and dump scheme creates artificial excitement for tokens and cryptocurrencies. Crypto and tokens are extremely vulnerable to this because they have low-trading volumes. Low-trading volumes are when the markets are thin and have few buy and sell offers. They are common in securities that have a market capitalization under US$2 billion. Most tokens and cryptocurrencies have market caps under US$500 million.

Many cryptocurrency exchanges and marketplaces support this behavior as they make money from the trading fees and selling the market data. In even more insidious cases, market operators would be pre-compensated with a token and then facilitate "wash trades". Think of this as chumming the water where bait is thrown into the water to attract fish. Issuers and exchange/market operator would create a fake volume of trades, making it look as if there was more demand for a token than there really was in the market. Other investors would then get sucked into buying the asset. Once the scam artist saw they had enough investors and natural trades, they would dump their tokens and crash the market.

On the flip side, because these markets had no real rules in place around the price you could offer to buy or sell a token, crafty individuals would push the market up or down through extra high prices or extra low prices. These extreme offers would cause chaos in the market, particularly because many investors used bots or preset buy and sales orders to help them trade. Traders do this because cryptocurrency exchanges operate globally, 24 hours a day seven days a week, so it is impossible for them to monitor the market at all times. In contrast, regulated exchanges operate in a single time zone and for a predefined number of hours and days a week.

The extremely low and extremely high prices would trigger buy-sell offers across the market causing depressions in value. A single individual could trigger these events, and exchanges and markets are still very vulnerable to this type of manipulation.

Pyramid and Ponzi schemes

Pyramid and "Ponzi" schemes are types of fraud that promise you high financial returns or dividends that are not available through traditional investments. In old school Ponzi schemes, the con artist will pay "dividends" to initial investors using the funds of subsequent investors. Often the con artist will not even invest the funds for the victims.

In the blockchain world, many ICOs looked a lot like Ponzi schemes. Con artists would list the tokens on exchanges and pump up the value through market manipulations. They would hire promoters who would talk about how great a project would be for the industry. Scam artists would put together a proposal for a new network or service that they would build once they received funds from investors. These proposals are often called "white papers". All of this activity would allow projects to have a veneer of legitimacy.

The top layers of the pyramid become rich, the bottom layers support the top participants.

Figure 35   Ponzi schemes – each layer of investors supports the next, allowing money to flow to those at the top.

There were some legitimate projects, but many were not. A simple way to distinguish between good projects and bad projects is to look at two things. The first thing to establish if the team has developed any part of the project. If the answer is no, then it's probably too risky to waste time with. The second factor to check is the experience of the team. In particular if they have built any similar technology.

10.4 Summary

Blockchain technology has come a long way. However, it is still under rapid development, and you must understand the limitations and challenges you will face. Both private and public blockchains can be manipulated and trusting blindly may well lead to disaster. Keep asking questions and staying curious, it will help you root out misinformation.

The transparency of transaction records and the self-clearing and settling nature of blockchain-backed financial instruments have made blockchain technology a fantastic innovation for the financial sector. However, as you have discovered in this chapter, transparent does not mean fraud-free. The same old tricks are still used to steal from and manipulate people.

Many individuals made life changing money investing in ICOs, but many more lost their entire investment. The speed, anonymity, and ease have attracted both innovators and fraudsters. Don't get carried away with pump and dump schemes or other investment opportunities that just don't make common sense. Investing as a practice is not any different in crypto and requires similar diligence as traditional investments.

10.5 Test your knowledge

1. **What was the most famous smart contract hacked?**
   A. DAO
   B. EOS
   C. Smart Contract Investment Fund
   D. ICO

2. **Do private blockchains mine cryptocurrency?**
   A. Yes
   B. No

3. **How did the Ethereum foundation resolve the hack of the DAO smart contract?**
   A. The Ethereum foundation edited the smart contract and returned investor funds.
   B. The Ethereum foundation did not fix the contract.
   C. The Ethereum foundation forked the network and created a new Ethereum.
   D. The hacker returned most of the funds.

4. **What is a 51% attack?**
   A. When a mining pool rotates between blockchain networks to optimize mining outcomes.
   B. When a government hacks a network.
   C. When 51% of the miners in the blockchain network agree to update the consensus algorithm.
   D. When the hash power of the network is controlled by one group and they use their control to manipulate the history of their blockchain.

5. **Are Proof of Work algorithms the only type of network structures that are vulnerable to 51% attacks?**
   A. Yes
   B. No

6. **How has the narcissism of small differences affected the blockchain community?**
   A. The blockchain community has grown closer and works together to solve problems.
   B. The community has developed many similar projects and these fight with one another over small differences.
   C. A group cares about small differences that can't be perceived by outside groups.
   D. One group makes fun of another group over small things.

7. **What is an "advanced fee scheme"?**
   A. A type of fraud where a con artist convinces an investor to invest in a new internet business.
   B. A type of fraud where a con artist convinces an investor to buy a new financial product that pays a dividend with a token.
   C. A type of fraud where a con artist convinces an investor to pay now for something that they anticipate will have greater value at a later time, but instead they receive something of little to no value.
   D. A type of fraud where a con artist convinces an investor to buy a registered security at a discount, but instead they receive something of value.

8. **What is a "sim card hack"?**
   A. Thieves use social engineering to gain access to your cell phone and personal records through a cellular provider.
   B. Thieves use social engineering to gain access to your email and social media accounts.
   C. Thieves use social engineering to gain access to your home and social group.
   D. Your phone is hacked through its Bluetooth.

9. **What is an ICO "pump and dump" scheme?**
   A. It is a type of securities fraud where banks dump poorly performing investments.
   B. It is a type of securities fraud where individuals create artificial excitement and buying pressure for tokens and cryptocurrencies.
   C. It is a type of securities fraud where rating firms exaggerate the value of a security.
   D. It is a type of securities fraud where individuals downplay risks for investors.

10. **What is a "Pyramid" scheme?**
    A. It is a type of securities fraud where insurance companies offer dividend-paying investment through financial planners.
    B. It is a type of securities fraud where issuers exaggerate the value of their offering and downplay the risk for investors.
    C. It is a type of securities fraud where a con artist steals the IP of another company.
    D. It is a type of securities fraud where a con artist promises high financial returns and supports those returns for a time by paying "dividends" to initial investors using the funds of subsequent investors.

Appendix A: Answer Keys

Section 1.3
1. C
2. D
3. A
4. C
5. D
6. D
7. A
8. B
9. C
10. D

Section 2.4
1. A
2. D
3. C
4. B
5. A
6. C
7. A
8. C
9. A
10. B

Section 3.10
1. A
2. D
3. C
4. B
5. B
6. C
7. A
8. D
9. C
10. A

Section 4.10
1. C
2. A
3. D
4. B
5. B
6. B
7. C
8. D
9. B
10. B
11. A
12. C
13. B
14. D

Section 5.6
1. C
2. B
3. D
4. A
5. B
6. A
7. B
8. D
9. A
10. B

Section 6.7
1. B
2. D
3. C
4. A
5. B
6. A
7. D
8. D
9. A
10. C

Section 7.5
1. C
2. A
3. B
4. D
5. C
6. A
7. B
8. C
9. A
10. D

Section 8.6
1. B
2. A
3. C
4. B
5. D
6. A
7. B
8. D
9. C
10. A

Section 9.16
1. C
2. B
3. A
4. C
5. B
6. A

Section 10.5
1. A
2. B
3. C
4. D
5. B
6. B
7. C
8. A
9. B
10. D

Index

-

51% attack   13, 25

A

AI (Artificial Intelligence)   83
American Payments Fraud & Control Survey   108
Andresen, Gavin   50
Aoki, Keith   121
API (application programming interface)   7
Artificial General Intelligence   93
ASIC mining chips   25
Assange, Julian   47
asymmetric cryptography   18
Avalon   26

B

B3i   120
BABB   117
Back, Adam   46
BCH (Bitcoin Cash)   50
Berne Convention (1886)   121
BIP (Bitcoin Improvement Proposal)   51
BIP 65 (Bitcoin Improvement Proposal)   72
Bitcoin   10, 47, 48
Bitcoin Obituaries   49
Bitcoin white paper (2008)   1
Bitlicense (New York Department of Financial Services)   139
Black Insurance   119
Bletchley Park   18
blockchain   4
    ~ledgers   18, 19
    ~network   45
    ~protected identity   85, 88
    ~technology   2
blockchain technology, second-generation applications   69
block headers   5
BlockRe   119
Blockstack   89

Blumer, Brendan   54
BTC (Bitcoin)   50
BTC mining   26
burning cryptocurrency   38
Buterin, Vitalik   59

C

CAC (Cyberspace Administration of China)   137
CBDC (Central Bank Digital Currency)   113
Central Bank Digital Money (Singapore)   136
centralized private networks   145
Chaincode (Hyperledger)   40
Chaincode Labs   51
ChainThat   120
channel   7
Chaum, David   46
China, Whole Country strategy   137
Civic, blockchain-based identity network   90
Clarke, Joan   18
Clayton, Jay   61
client   5
competitive governance   129
consensus system   5
Corda   6
Corda (R3)   109
COTI (FinTech company)   109
credit card fraud   147
cryptocurrency   9
cryptography   17
Cryptokitties   11
Cypherpunk   47

D

DAO (Decentralized Autonomous Organization)   76, 144
DApps (decentralized applications)   32, 46, 74

dark pools   147
DCI (Digital Currency Initiative)   51
decentralized identity   83
decentralized marketplace   94
Delegated Proof of Stake (DPoS)   34
DEX (Waves Decentralized Exchange)   63
DIF (Decentralized Identity Foundation)   89
Diffie, Whitfield   18
Digicash   9, 46
digital collectibles   11
digital fiat currency   113
digital IP   122
digital reproduction   122
DLT (distributed ledger technology)   6, 27, 51, 84
DPoS (Delegated Proof of Stake)   54

E

economic incentivization   12
eCurrency   116
electronic data notarization services (China)   131
Elixxir   46
encryption   17
Enigma   17, 94
EOA (externally owned accounts)   72
EOS   53
ePOD (Electronic Proof of Delivery)   104
ERC-20 token standard   11, 59, 73
ERC-72 token standard   11
ERC-721 token standard   73
e-Residency (Estonia)   130
Ethereum   59
Ethereum Academic and Research Collaboration   61
Ethereum blockchain   11
Ethereum Classic   144
Ethereum foundation   11
Everex (FinTechn company)   109
Everledger   104

F

Factoids   9
Factom federated network   9
Falke, Marco   51
federated blockchain nodes   8
federated Factom nodes   8
FinCEN   56
FinTech industry   114
fork   33
Franklin, Benjamin   118
Fugger, Ryan   55
full node   4

G

GBA (Global Blockchain Council), UEA   139
GitHub   96
Global Blockchain Survey 2019 (Deloitte)   47
gold standard   22

H

hackathons   61
hardfork   24
Hashcash   46
hashes   2, 19
Hellman, Martin E.   18
Hinman, William   61
hybrid blockchains   12
Hyperledger Composer   53
Hyperledger Fabric   7, 39, 51
Hyperledger Fabric Node   40

I

IBM, Trusted Identity solution   89
ICANN (Internet Corporation for Assigned Names and Numbers)   48
ICO (initial coin offering)   11
ID2020 Alliance   89
identity of citizens   86
Identity Overlay Network Infrastructure   89
identity theft   147
identity verification   87

IETF (Internet Engineering Task Force) 48
IMAP (Internet Message Access Protocol) 48
Insurance industry 117
intellectual property rights 121
IoT (Internet of Things) 38, 90
IPwe 123
Ivanov, Sacha 62

K
Knights Templar 22

L
Laan, Wladimir J. van der 51
Larimer, Daniel 54
ledger 6, 21, 45
legal contracts 70
legal identity 87
lightweight nodes 5
Liquid 116
LOCI 123
Luhn, Hans Peter 19

M
machine learning 93
Madrid Agreement (1891) 121
Malta Digital Innovation Authority Act 140
market manipulation 148
MAS (Monetary Authority of Singapore) 107
MDIA (Malta Digital Innovation Authority) 79
Medici family 105
mempools 50
Merkle tree root 14
Microsoft, distributed ledger platform on Azure 89
miner 5
mining 4, 24
MIT Media Lab 51, 92
MSA (Monetary Authority of Singapore) 136

N
Nakamoto, Satoshi 1, 10, 31, 47
NFC (Near-Field Communication) 103
node 4
nonce 6
nothing-at-stake problem 33
Nxt (Proof-of-Stake protocol) 62

O
online chat rooms 86
OpenPort 104
OPN (OpenPorts Token) 104
orderer peers 7

P
Paris Convention (1883) 121
passport 86
PayPal 106
Peers and Orderers 7
Peertracks 134
Perelman, Or 59
permissioned blockchains 6
PlatON 135
Ponzi scheme 149
private blockchains 12
private key 2, 19
Proof of Authority (PoA) 35
Proof of Burn 38
Proof-of-Capacity (PoC) 37
Proof of Elapsed Time (PoET) 36
Proof-of-Space (PoSpace) 37
Proof of Stake (PoS) 33
Proof of Work (PoW) 31, 46
Proof of Work (PoW) public blockchains 144
public blockchains 6, 12
public-key cryptography 18
public witness 22
pyramid scheme 149

R
R3 Consortium 109
R3 platform 6
RCN (Ripio Credit Network) 116

RFID (Radio Frequency IDentification)   103
Ripple   55
Ripple protocol   108

S

Sawtooth Lake project   36
secret key   17
SEC (Securities and Exchange Commission)   60
security of online data   87
SegWit (Segregated Witness)   51
self-sovereign identity   85
SendFriend   110
SHA256 (Secure Hashing Algorithm 256)   20
ShipChain   104
Silk Road   49
sim card hacks   148
Simplified Payment Verification (SPV)   5
Singapore SMart Nation project   136
SingularityNET   94
smart cities   135
smart contracts   69, 143
Smart Dubai initiative   138
Spoofing   90
STO (Security tokens)   74
Strong AI   93
supply chain industry   101
SwiftMail   132
SWIFT (Society for Worldwide Interbank Financial Telecommunication)   105
Szabo, Nick   70

T

TEE (trusted execution environment)   36
Todd, Peter   72
tokens   10
tokens, second generation   74
token standards   73
Toyota Research Institute   92
transaction   21
trust   87
trusted authorship   133
Turing, Alan   18

U

UjoMusic   134

V

Vaultitude   124
Ver, Roger   56

W

Waves platform   62
Waves (public blockchain)   9
Weak AI   92
Western Union   106
Wikileaks   47
WIPO (World Intellectual Property Organization)   121
witnesses   34
Woorton   116
Wuille, Pieter   51

X

XRP (Ripple)   55

Y

Yifu Guo   26

Index